THE GASPING CITY

RECONNECTING WITH NATURE
NEW HISTORIES

JADAVPUR UNIVERSITY
HISTORY MONOGRAPH SERIES

Other titles in this series:

River, Society and Culture: Environmental Perspectives on the Rivers of Assam and Bengal
RUP KUMAR BARMAN

Indian Medicinal Plants in the Shifting Terrains of Science: Botanical and Medical Literature of Nineteenth-century Bengal
NUPUR DASGUPTA

Rethinking Human–Animal Relationship: Reading Stories from Bengali Literature
ANURADHA ROY

The Gasping City

AN ENVIRONMENTAL HISTORY OF CALCUTTA, 1817–1923

Mahua Sarkar

PRIMUS BOOKS
An imprint of Ratna Sagar P. Ltd.
Virat Bhavan
Mukherjee Nagar Commercial Complex
Delhi 110 009

Offices at CHENNAI LUCKNOW AGRA AHMEDABAD BENGALURU BHOPAL COIMBATORE DEHRADUN GUWAHATI HYDERABAD JAIPUR JALANDHAR KANPUR KOCHI KOLKATA MUMBAI PATNA RANCHI VARANASI

First published 2023

ISBN: 978-93-5687-836-5 (Paperback)
ISBN: 978-93-5687-071-0 (POD)

Published by Primus Books

Laser typeset by Jojy Philip
jojyphilip@gmail.com

Contents

Foreword

The research programme on environmental history of South Asia was initiated in the Department of History, Jadavpur University, under the University Grants Commission's Special Assistance Programme (SAP) in 2004. I had the privilege to head the programme during its first two phases. This programme was the first of its kind in the country. This centre for environmental history gradually earned recognition both within the country and beyond. The faculty members of the department have already published quite an impressive number of books and articles on the subject. Such publications grew out of the several SAP-funded research projects undertaken at our centre. A large number of international and national conferences, on various themes of environmental history, were organized and the department also hosted about twenty outstanding scholars in the field as visiting professors. I have already mentioned in my edited volumes *Situating Environmental History* (2007, new edn., 2021) and *Critical Themes in Environmental History of India* (2020) and in my recent monograph, *Climate, Calamity and the Wild* (Primus Books, 2022) that though environmental history is one of the most important areas of enquiry in the field of history, it still remains as a less explored field without well-defined disciplinary standards and methodological strategies. It is felt that professional historians with the requisite methodological training will be able to (a) develop and define the agenda and disciplinary canons of this field of inquiry, and (b) historicize the present-day concerns and anxieties in the broad area of environmental history.

In his recent book *The Climate of History in a Planetary Age* (Primus Books, 2021), Dipesh Chakrabarty argues that historians need to revise many of their fundamental assumptions and methodologies in this period of human-induced climate change. While confronting environmental issues today, when globalization has triggered the threat of global warming and mass extinction, historians are inventing new conceptual categories to integrate questions that they have usually treated in the past as separate and virtually unconnected. This finds manifestation in the recent rise of the term 'environmental humanities'. It is an interdisciplinary umbrella category that accommodates environmental history, environmental philosophy, cultural geography, ecocriticism, cultural anthropology, political and social ecology and so on. Humans have been engaged in a meaningful intellectual dialogue with the earth as a category since the post-Second World War period, but the planet as a category was not visible earlier. Now, under the threat of global warming, humans have come face to face with planetary categories as well, aided by post-humanist scholars like Bruno Latour. This marks the beginning of a communicative relationship between humans and the planet. Now the way has been paved for the emergence of the planet as a historical category. The formalized emergence of planetary humanities as another useful conceptual category is just a matter of time. Historians need to connect deep and recorded histories and establish conversational links between the historical time and geological and biological times. This will enable the historians to tell the larger story of how a particular biological species, Homo sapiens, along with its Technosphere, as well as other species that co-evolved with or were dependent on them, came to dominate the entire planet within a short span of time.

The human–nature interface has been the most fundamental issues in whatever decisions human society has taken since time immemorial. One of the aspects of the inner conflicts within human societies of the past was fuelled by the continuous effort to resolve the question relating to the legitimate use of the natural world. As human settlements spread across the earth and as technology advanced, the urge to resolve this fundamental question intensified. An overarching denial of this issue by humankind, armed with the Technosphere, especially in recent decades, has completely disrupted the natural balance of the planet. It is now the final call for historians to address and resolve this fundamental question. The connection between the legitimate use of natural world and its connection with power and profit has put environmental issues on an equal footing with historical categories like race, class, gender, ethnicity, and nationalism. However, even in the face of a growing environmental crisis, humanity has shown a kind of indifference to environmental issues while giving more emphasis to power and politics. The present series, like many others in recent years, urge historians to reorient minds to the need of the hour, i.e. concern for Planet Earth.

The present series 'Reconnecting with the Nature' contains four different monographs: Rup Kumar Barman's *River, Society and Culture: Environmental Perspectives on the Rivers of Assam and Bengal*; Nupur Dasgupta's *Indian Medicinal Plants in the Shifting Terrains of Science: Botanical and Medical Literature of Nineteenth-century Bengal*; Anuradha Roy's *Rethinking Human–Animal Relationship: Reading Stories from Bengali Literature*; and Mahua Sarkar's *The Gasping City: An Environmental History of Calcutta, 1817–1923* is the outcome of a commendable effort towards re-establishing the human–nature interface.

River, Society and Culture: Environmental Perspectives on the Rivers of Assam and Bengal critically analyses the migration crisis and river–human relationships. The discourse offers an understanding of the lesser-explored society and culture of the Titash-Tista-Kalahi-Raidak basins of Bengal, Assam, and Bhutan from an environmental perspective. *Indian Medicinal Plants in the Shifting Terrains of Science: Botanical and Medical Literature of Nineteenth-century Bengal* traces the processes of medical and botanical reconnaissance during the nineteenth century, with a focus on indigenous medicinal plants, and also observes their integration into the framework of modern science. In *Rethinking Human–Animal Relationship: Reading Stories from Bengali Literature*, the author argues that animal studies should be considered a growing interdisciplinary field. The historiography of this field shows a 'moral schizophrenia' of human beings towards animal 'others'. It further seeks to connect the unrelenting exploitation of animals throughout history to the domination of humans by humans—oppression of women, racial and community struggles, etc. Finally, *The Gasping City: An Environmental History of Calcutta, 1817–1923* begins with an explanation of the intricate relationship between the development of cityscapes and its impact on the surrounding environment. Set between the period of 1817 and 1923, it also analyses the responses and attitudes of the educated urban people to ongoing environmental changes. Whether the traits of a 'planned city' was compatible or incompatible with the sustainable growth of environment is the main thrust area of this monograph.

With the publication of the present series— 'Reconnecting with Nature'—I have no doubt that the immense potentials and possibilities of environmental history will be further refurbished. The grand quest to reach a resolution pertaining to the legitimate use of nature, I believe, will continue to dominate the discipline of history and its related knowledge systems. Environmental histories and environmental humanities will continue to thrive because the seeds of a new social and cultural history are firmly embedded in it. The importance of the present series has to be understood in this broader context.

RANJAN CHAKRABARTI

Note on the Series

Could history have been made without nature as the nurturing site for living species, without the primordial bounty of water, flora, and fauna? How did the hominids create their own space in this, the rarest of planets in the known orbit of the universe? How well have we been able to attain and preserve this? Can we sustain this with the progression of 'civilization' as we understand it? These are fundamental matters in environmental studies today and the questions take us beyond the rigidly defined contours of the discipline of history, which was specifically built around the human species. History is now observed to include much wider frames and perspectives.

The Department of History, Jadavpur University, is the first academic institution in the country to begin running a UGC-sponsored DRS Project on the History of Environment, with Professor Ranjan Chakravarti as the coordinator, from 2005. He successfully built the foundations of the discipline in the department. Within a decade, the programme achieved the level of a UGC DSA-I Special Assistance Project in 2015. The project has then been steered successively by Professor Amit Bhattacharya and Professor Mahua Sarkar. I was put in charge in 2018 and have supervised the programme till its completion in 2020. The department has witnessed a long tradition of research in the history of environment and allied subjects. The last few years from 2018 to 2020 saw a fresh bout of research by the faculty. The proposal for the publication of a few such research works was approved by the authorities of Jadavpur University in 2019–20. The outcome is showcased in the present series of books. The series consists of four short monographs, each devoted to a different theme, embodying distinct areas of research under the overarching theme of environmental history. The authors focus on elemental nature and human life around it. Thus, rivers, flora, fauna, and ecology in the urban context have been chosen as the major sites of investigation. The discussions here are distinctly designed to present new perspectives. An inkling of the overall philosophy of research has been briefly raised above. The authors, in their various contexts and approaches, project the deeper urge of the historian to illuminate the profundity of the existence of life on the Blue Planet. This short note to the series does not intend to delve any deeper into the themes and the underlying concerns they present. These have been discussed in detail in the authors' respective Introductions to their books.

I end this note by extending my thanks to those without whose support we could not have run the programme nor would this series have seen the light of day. First and foremost, I am beholden to the Hon'ble Vice-Chancellor of Jadavpur University, Professor Suranjan Das, for constant academic inspiration and advice. My sincerest thanks go to him and the authorities of the university for providing all the facilities required for carrying out the long-term project in the Department of History. I must express my deepest gratitude to all my colleagues in the department and outside it for their unstinted support. I am indebted to Professor Ranjan Chakrabarti, Professor Amit Bhattacharya, and Professor Mahua Sarkar, who were extremely generous in offering help and advice in running the programme and in carrying out the task of publications. Professor Anuradha Roy and Professor Rup Kumar Barman have been ready with all suggestions and help about the publication process. Sri Hemendranath Mandal, Sri Bholanath Mandal, and Sri Ritwik Bagchi, the research assistants associated with the programme, deserve high praise for helping me to carry out my duties throughout these years. The office staff, the librarians, and the library staff of the department have been extremely helpful and diligent in providing all support. I am ever so grateful for that. Finally, we owe much to our publishers, Primus Books, for ready support and for keeping us on schedule. I especially thank Mr B.N. Varma for showing interest in the project. Dr Prasun Chatterjee has extended great support through the process of publication, without which our project might have languished. I would like to extend profuse thanks to Ms Jyotika Mansata for taking the utmost care in preparing the manuscripts. Finally, I acknowledge with the deepest gratitude our indebtedness to the University Grants Commission for making it possible for the whole project and this series to come to fruition.

Nupur Dasgupta

Acknowledgements

This monograph is an environmental history of nineteenth and early twentieth century Calcutta. In the context of science, health, sanitation, and construction, this book explores the background of two conflicting political processes: the demand for an integrated, controlled development chalked out by an elite group of colonial scientists, technicians and businessman, and the demand for a looser system allowing indigenous elites to have a voice through elected government representatives. This is perhaps one of the final attempts of the UGC Departmental Special Assistance scheme run by the Department of History, Jadavpur University since 2005, to proliferate its activities in academia. We are grateful to Professor Suranjan Das, Honourable Vice-Chancellor of our university, for constantly encouraging us to publish our research. Our DSA programme has successfully organized national and international seminars and published the researches of our guests and faculties. I thank Professor Ranjan Chakrabarti and Professor Amit Bhattacharya, our previous coordinators, for organizing the DSA programme. With their assistance I have been able to publish three edited volumes on environmental history as the third coordinator of the scheme. I am grateful to Professor Nupur Dasgupta, our present coordinator, for the publication of this monograph. I thank all my colleagues for all their assistance. I am grateful to the publisher of this volume and also acknowledge how grateful I am to my students.

Mahua Sarkar

Introduction

This work is the first attempt to write a city's environmental history from the perspectives of the development of science, planning of structures, and health and sanitation in the mid-nineteenth and early twentieth centuries. It is located in a time when the colonial government started funding the moral and material development of the city and ends before the direct political demand raised by the Swarajya Party to participate in the developmental and municipal affairs of the colonial state. The city in question is colonial Calcutta. I will start with the foundation of the Lottery Committee in 1817, by which the municipal improvement of the city was initiated. This period saw the emergence of associational politics, cultural nationalism and the Swadeshi movement in Bengal. Mahatma Gandhi had not yet appeared in the political scenario of Bengal. This was a time when earlier zeal for social reform was gradually dying out in the face of the partition of Bengal in 1905 and the transfer of the capital from Calcutta to Delhi in 1911. The most important changes to the city were effected under the Act of 1923, when Surendranath Banerjea was the minister for local self-government. The Act liberalized the constitution of the Calcutta

Corporation along democratic lines. The adjacent municipalities of Cossipore, Chitpur, and Manicktala were amalgamated into Calcutta in this year. A large area adjacent to Calcutta was thus included within the limits of the corporation. Women were also enfranchised by this Act. Under the Act of 1923, the first Mayor, Deputy Mayor, and Chief Executive Officer were Chittaranjan Das, Subhas Chandra Bose, and Huseyn Shaheed Suhrawardy, respectively. Meanwhile the grip of the vernacular press was expanding and new themes of health, sanitation, and cleanliness were repeatedly coming up in the discourses of the Bengali people. The idea of a model clean place like Chowringhee was also perceived by the bhadralok of Calcutta. They taught their female counterparts (i.e. the bhadramahila) Western methods of sanitation and childcare but were unsure of adopting such methods for a modern, clean city. The government acted promptly, with the new Building Commission formally set up in 1876 and the Calcutta Improvement Trust in 1911. New roads were built and vaccination camps were organized. Did these new ventures serve the purposes of the bhadralok or did the city end up a jungle of concrete and slums? At what point did the urban environment become corrupt with pollution and what triggered this? Was Calcutta a planned city from the very beginning? Perhaps unaware of the term 'environment', how did the bhadralok and bhadramahila respond to the structural development, health, and sanitation in the city of palaces? I have sought to find answers to some of these questions from primary, official, and vernacular sources.

First, let me explain the term 'environmental history', after which I shall discuss Calcutta and its environmental crisis on a historical plane. 'Environmental history' was not, until recently, a frequently used expression and it has not been as fully institutionalized, academically and pedagogically, like other branches of history. The retreat from faith in impartial 'truth' or a linear history of progress to the desire to bring the past nearer to the boundaries of people's lives and problems, has stimulated an attempt to direct the corpus of the past under the category of newer genres. In fact, the human world and the notion of development itself have stood at a critical juncture in recent times. There is now a widespread belief that no resource is finite. This fear of a dying world has given rise to the development of a new field of knowledge called environmental studies; no branch of knowledge is complete without its history. To have a constant dialogue between the past and the present, the study of environmental history has become very important.[1] The genesis of environmental history in the late 1960s arose out of political and intellectual history. The genre took shape largely from two relevant works published in the USA, namely Samuel P. Hays's *Conservation and the Gospel of Efficiency* and Roderick Nash's *Wilderness and the American Mind*.[2] What made these two books more than just major works in their pre-existing fields was the contemporary rise of the environment movement. Environment problems reached a new urgency in the 1960s and 1970s and environmental activists attained a political prominence that could not be ignored. But since its inception, the field has become very complex.

Historians defined environment exclusively in terms of wilderness or, at least, unsettled land. Approaches to environmental history also have so far been guided by two broad paradigms of human-nature relations. If one is the key construction of nature and culture through history, the other is what has been broadly defined as political ecology.[3] Both these paradigms have been criticized and modified by historians. The focus of this essay is to address the relevance of these concepts by examining the place of the city in environmental history. Two important trajectories generally arise within this central theme. The first takes into account the excessive importance attached to the natural rural landscape and forest issues; the second is the overlooking of environmental issues in favour of urban history in general.

Indeed, the place of the city in environmental history is largely ill-defined.[4] The study of the environment focuses on the role of the humane in the natural world and rarely encompasses the city. The study of the 'urban' remains confined to the realm of technology and culture. Long before the field of urban environmental history was established, geographers had begun to explore the connections between the city and the environment; their attention was focused on the city's natural physical characteristics and dimensions. A noted scholar, Graeme Davidson, wrote about the city itself as a natural system. He argues that though akin to nature, the city stood apart from nature and reflected man's own ambiguous relationship to the natural order.[5] The idea of the city as a natural system has never gained universal appeal but it created graphic biological metaphors relating the structure and operation of the city to that of the human body. Such a theory stimulates images of community interdependency and the rational functioning of the city's many components. In an article titled 'The Problematic Nature of Nature: the Post-Constructivist Challenge to Environmental History', Kristin Asdal discusses the programme of environmental history within the larger discipline of history and contrasts it with more recent contributions from post-structuralist science.[6] She explores the ways in which post-structuralism has the potential to productively address many of the problems of environmental history's theories and models that environmental historians themselves have begun to view with a critical eye. She refers to post-structuralist authors like Donna Haraway and Bruno Latour who have challenged the ways in which nature and the natural sciences tend to be conceptualized as non-problematized entities within environmental history. These scholars also challenge the ways in which dichotomies of nature and culture tend to be reproduced within the programme of environmental history.[7] It is argued that these post-structuralist contributions represent a radical and more truly historical way of introducing non-human actors into the historical narrative, and thus represent a potential reinvigoration of environmental history that would embrace a more radical historicity, greater diversity, and openness to theories of power.[8] Asdal informs us that Michel Foucault (1984) raised this point in his short essay 'What is Enlightenment?', which focused on the work of Immanuel Kant and the role of critique as a way of transcending the discursive limits imposed on us by history.[9] Historically, Foucault defines Enlightenment as the age of the critique.[10] His understanding of disciplinary power was to interrogate the micro-political processes of social control at work inside behaviour change interventions.[11] Through it, action by individuals comes to be seen as the most appropriate solution to global environmental issues.[12] The role of the individuals and collective agencies become important in environmental history in the issue of transformation of resources. In his book, Spenser Havlick states that a city or town is a transformed combination of resources (land, water, air, mineral, human) and that the major goal of urbanization is to convert resource bases into cities.[13] The eminent sociologist David Harvey remarked that an urban system is a giant man-made resource system. He suggests that the growth of a city involves the structuring and differentiation of space through the distribution of fixed capital investments.[14] All these scholars define the city as a construct dependent on reordering natural resources to form a new order. While this argument goes beyond basic assumptions of the city as a natural system, it nonetheless continues to embrace the organic nature of cities. Another expert, Manuel Castells, places more emphasis on human action in structuring cities and also perceives cities as dynamic rather than static. To him, cities are living systems, made, transformed and experienced by people.[15] Urban forms and functions are produced and managed by the interaction between space and society, i.e. by the historical relationship between human consciousness, matter, energy, and information. Two famous geographers, Thomas R. Detwyler and Melvin

G. Marcus, view the city as a relatively new kind of ecosystem on the face of the earth. It is an open system not functioning independently or in isolation from the rest of the world.[16]

These views are all modifications of the organic theory but are still rooted in it. Cities are, thus, not static backdrops for human actions, nor are they mere organic metaphors. They are ever-changing built-in systems that themselves modify the physical environment. Their existence influences the course of basic physical processes such as the hydraulic cycle. Urbanization rapidly stimulates precipitation into existing watercourses or flooding and removes much of the filtering capacity of the soil. City building affects the atmosphere by increasing air-borne pollutants and creating 'heat islands' where temperatures are greater than the surrounding area. Various urban activities produce huge volumes of waste products that require complex disposal mechanisms. The urban ecosystem seldom returns air and water resources to the ecosphere in the same condition in which they are received. On the other hand, cities have the capacity to use resources more efficiently than highly decentralized populations in rural areas. Cities, if properly designed, may contain the hub of a proper environmental policy suitable for sustainable development.[17] The theory of this urban ecology can be traced to the nineteenth century concepts conceived by plant and animal ecologists. During World War I, Robert E. Park and Ernest Burgess led this 'Subsocial School' in the University of Chicago, which studied man in his temporal and spatial dimensions with variables like impersonal competition and crime.[18] Since the 1950s, a theory of community structure emerged in the field of urban ecology. All these theories are significant to an environmental historian, who should examine external as well as internal influences shaping the growth and development of an urban environ. Sociologists, geographers, and other social scientists have made valuable contributions in this field, which very few historians have attempted to confront in broader environmental terms. The primary focus of much of the existing research has been internalist, narrow, and empirical rather than broad and theoretical in nature. Ian Douglas wrote about the city as a dependent system with regard to food, raw materials, and water supplies, the acquisition of which has significant environmental impacts. He suggested that cities should encompass a number of balances, including those pertaining to energy, water, geochemicals, waste material disposal, geographical aspect of urban health and diseases, and the reduction of environmental hazards.[19] While urban environmental historians have begun to explore some of the categories set out by Douglas two decades ago, major gaps still exist. These gaps are related to the physical circumstances of the city, including its geomorphology and hydrology, natural history, climate, materials, and food. These are the domains where scientists and social scientists have been providing important insights. These emphasize the necessity of approaching urban environmental history from an interdisciplinary perspective. While some environmental historians have commented that a material and systems approach to study urban environmental history often leaves out the human element, it is not always so. The material structure of the city is intimately connected with many aspects of its social and community life. It is essential that urban environmental historians understand this structure in order to comprehend those relationships. Environmental history could serve to demonstrate the multitude of ways in which the urban environment affects and shapes city life. For a historian studying a colonized region, the work of Lewis Mumford is important in this context. Though not strictly an urban ecologist, Mumford views the complex problem of an urban society as products of an imbalance between nature and culture. He has correctly noticed the existence of cities within cities.[20] The pattern of growth in a colonial city obviously produces a core area with peripheries within a single city as well as a core city with dependable suburbs surrounding it.

Coming to what we call 'thick history', the present volume refers to the environmental history of early colonial Calcutta and the ecological reasons for selecting this site. This marshy area, close to the mangrove forests of the Sundarbans and the Bay of Bengal, lying at the southernmost tip of the Bengal Delta, offered a unique landscape with two minute riverine systems—the Hooghly in the west and the Bidyadhari in the east. The nomenclature 'Calcutta' is itself a reflection of its hydraulic topography, though there are debates regarding the source of its name. Calcutta is said to have been originally made up of 3 villages: Kolikata lay in the centre with Sutanuti to the north and Govindapur to the south. The middle portion was marked by indentations in the coastline because of creeks and inlets. To denote this, a Bengali word was used: *'kolkata'*, *kol* means 'shore' and *kata* meaning 'cut open'. The two words together imply a coast or shore cut open by creeks or canals. Near the southern limit of Calcutta there was a 'deep miry gully' running from Chandpal ghat to Balliaghat near Salt Lake. The creek was named Creek Row or *Dinga Bhanga* in Bengali, which originated after the wrecking of ship there during the terrible cyclone of 1737, mentioned in the writing of H. Blochmann in the nineteenth century. The presence of another canal flowing eastward along the northern boundary is reflected in the existence of the term '*Jora-Sanko*', which means 'joint river-bridge'. There were many other canals and bridges throughout the area and Bengali names like Sealdah(a), Ultadanga and Beliaghata suggest the existence of shores and waterbodies in Calcutta. With the river Hooghly on the left, and the Bidyadhari and the Adi Ganga on the right the existence of the city and its port could be based on the natural linkages through water channels. Rivers, with an outlet to the sea, were the best means of communication, connecting Howrah, Hooghly, 24 Parganas, Khulna, Faridpur, Bakharganj, and Barisal, carrying the produce of East Bengal and the Brahmaputra valley to Calcutta and vice versa. Hence, from the eighteenth century, an ecological dynamic controlled and influenced settlement in this region. The British merchants had a deep-rooted vision to extract raw materials and surplus capital from the area, to make it a heterogenetic centre of urban growth, and to transform Calcutta into the seat of an imperial capital (that is, until it shifted in 1911–12).[21] Calcutta is located in a low alluvial plain, slightly elevated above sea level, within the lower orbit of the Ganges Delta. From a geological point of view, it is of the Miocene Age. Geologists seem to agree that Calcutta was once a part of the extensive Sundarbans. The discovery of forests of submerged *sundari* trees in at least five different natural swamps around the city provide convincing proof, and these date back at least 5,000 years. Historical meteorological data indicate an average rainfall of 66.04 in. and the atmospheric pressure was 29,7039 p.a.) in early colonial Calcutta. It is located at 22° 35' north and 88° 21' east on the left bank of the river Hooghly about 36 km. before the river debouches into the Bay of Bengal. Rainey's *Historical and Topographical Sketch of Calcutta* of 1876 covers the chronological ecology of the city from 1690, the year in which Job Charnock arrived in the village of Sutanuti on 24 August. The city was finally borne out of three villages, as mentioned earlier: Govindapur, Kolikata, and Sutanuti. The former was towards the south and commenced at what is now called Tolly's Nala (Govindapur Creek) and extended northward to the sight of Fort William, while the latter was to the north and began at what is now called Chitpur Canal or *Baghbazar Khal*, where the Maratha Ditch was dug later; Kolikata was located in between the two villages. The three villages, approximately 5 km. in area, were bought by the East India Company for a sum of Rs.1300. With the appointment of Warren Hastings as the first Governor General of India in 1774, Calcutta became the focal point of the growing British Empire; it was the second-largest jewel in its crown. A letter sent from London to Bengal dated March 1695 stated, 'Chuttanutty to be the station in Bengal', for 'Chuttanutty where our ships ride well and where we are in a great measure already settled.'[22] The ecological advantages that the site offered to the British can be summed up briefly. It was closer to the sea than Hooghly and hence could provide better trading facilities. It was situated on the eastern bank of the river and was strategically more secure from attacks by Mughals and the Marathas. The Hooghly River tapped the trade of the Ganges valley and Sutanuti was situated at the highest point at which the river was navigable for sea-going vessels. It had easy communication with Bihar, Orissa, and other parts of Bengal. The Ganges and the southern creeks could be used for trade between Calcutta and present-day Bangladesh. On the eastern side, the city was protected from invasion by the presence of extensive salt lakes. Cost of land acquisition and settlement were cheaper as the place was marshy and swampy. Yet, this was not an area of howling wilderness, because it was already inhabited by the Seths and Basaks, agriculturists, small traders, and fishermen. The advantages in terms of defense and services were effectual to overbalance its disadvantages. Eight years after the foundation of British Calcutta, in 1698, the agents of the Company wrote that it was 'the Best Money ever spent'.[23] This story can be referred to as the victory of the site over situation. The riverine topography of the area provided a utility with the requirement of few initiatives that the colonizers eyes did not miss foreseeing. That was why the city of Calcutta evolved from a small trading post during the early eighteenth century to a bustling city by the mid-nineteenth century. Since the early nineteenth century, the city witnessed huge industrial investments by the British and their Indian agents in jute, textiles, chemicals, heavy engineering, cement, pharmaceuticals, food processing, leather, and metallurgical studies. Calcutta came to be recognized as one of the most important commercial and industrial hubs in Asia. The industrialization was followed by rapid urbanization. The economic opportunities that followed this led to massive influx of population from the interior villages of the province and from the neighbouring areas of Bihar, Orissa, and the north-eastern parts of the country. With the growth of urbanization, the city experienced a steady decline in its ecological balance due to the unkempt expansion of habitation. Right from the beginning, Calcutta witnessed a haphazard growth, without any concern for its environment. The city was developed into different quarters or patterns of settlement: the white town of the Europeans, the black town of the zamindars, the intermediate zones, and the innumerable slums of the common people, differentiated by caste, community, and ethnicity. The rural nature of the landscape and society was retained throughout the nineteenth century and the colonial masters did not bother providing civic amenities to the people. The politics of power and profit led to considerable strain on the natural environment of Calcutta. The messy format of urbanization had an evil impact on the natural sewage system. The East Calcutta Wetlands, which worked as the lungs of the city, began to be sealed up by newly established habitation, and the canals were not upgraded or maintained keep pace with rapid urbanization. As a result, Calcutta began to face substantial urban pollution, traffic congestion, poverty, overpopulation, deplorable conditions of public health, unorganized housing, and other logistic and socio-economic problems. This tragic episode began from the early twentieth century and the situation has not changed even today.

The dynamic characteristics of an urban nature added an ambiguous dimension to the city's surrounding ecology. The term 'pollution' is spatially, individually, publicly as well as socially constructed. This notion is not only a modern invocation but can also be traced back to the age of the Mangalkavyas, when the 'pure' castes were aware of mingling with the 'impure' castes. However, the idea of pollution received a new dimension with the advent of Western conceptions of science and public health, incorporating new ideas about disease, cleanliness, and sanitation. Throughout the late nineteenth and early twentieth centuries, the British made concrete efforts towards dispensing Western medicine and sense of cleanliness in hospitals and dispensaries, promoting vaccination for smallpox, controlling cholera and other diseases, and implementing sanitary schemes for water supply, drainage, and conservancy. If we consider vernacular sources along with official texts, then a multicoloured picture of urbanity is evident. The omnipresent issue of a growing environmental crisis within the story of colonial urbanization can also be addressed from this varied rubric. From the very beginning, the colonial encounter proved to be geographically advantageous for Calcutta as the government chose this place as their administrative headquarters. There are a large number of writings on the history of Calcutta as its uniqueness was quite attractive to historians, chroniclers, and obviously to colonial administrators. But earlier writers have concentrated more on the origin, growth, and description of the old city. Both colonial writers, such as H. Beverly, H.E. Busteed, and H.E.A Cotton, and Indian writers such as Radharaman Mitra, Bhabanicharan Bandyopadhyay, Sivanath Sastri, and, later, P.T. Nair, S.N. Mukherjee, Asok Mitra, and N.K. Bose, were pioneers in creating the legacy of writing the city's history.[24] The growth of the city through the nineteenth and early twentieth centuries has been well documented through various monumental works. A.K Roy's *History of Calcutta* is one such important contribution. Pradip Sinha is one of the prominent historians to write on the social history of Calcutta. The recent works of Partho Datta, Debjani Bhattacharya, and Swati Chattopadhyay on planning, environment, and architecture of the city are also worth mentioning.[25] Sumanta Banerjee has portrayed an exquisite picture of the city's expansion into global megalopolis through the encroachment of suburbs in the name of building roads.[26] Earlier, he also wrote on the elite and marginal cultures and criminalization of the chotolok of Calcutta. Anindita Ghosh, in her seminal work on Calcutta, brings forth the complications inherent in assuming the nature of the city either from the narratives of glorified British administrators or from the passivity of the Bengalis.[27] Earlier studies by scholars like Anthony D. King talked about the protracted growth of a colonial city under the British government where the growth model supplemented the social control policy of the colonial rulers.[28] Indeed, within the colonial structure, the term 'development' was used in a nuanced way. Dipesh

Chakrabarty has used the term, 'hyperreal Europe' to denote the construction of 'Europe' in the everyday life of the colonized people.[29] These scholars, studying the planning and development of Calcutta, have paid significant attention to the various ideas, intellectual currents and notions about the environment, the city, the tropics, and the resultant health issues that formed this discourse. As for the history of science, the imperialist schools of historians think that the core, i.e. Western science and medicine of the colonizing country completely regulated the impact of Western research in the peripheries or the colonies. Deepak Kumar, on the other hand, has critically reviewed the relationship between science and imperialism from various aspects in his pioneering work on *Science and the Raj* as well as in later publications.[30] Scholars like Mark Harrison also argue that Western medicine in India had its own typical uniqueness and many other academics are now highlighting the importance of the peripheries or the micro-local in the history of medicine.[31] Various historians have written on the history of public health in India. The works of David Arnold, Mark Harrison, Roger Jeffrey, Deepak Kumar, Biswamoy Pati, Radhika Ramasubban, Poonam Bala, etc., for example are worth mentioning.[32] Kabita Ray, in her *History of Public Health: Colonial Bengal* (1998), has studied colonial health policies and the Indian reactions to them from 1921 to 1947; from this she can provide us with a significant detailed narrative on medicine in colonial Bengal.[33] Srirupa Prasad writes on the cultural politics of hygiene in India between 1890 and 1940.[34] Pratik Chakrabarti, in his book on bacteriology in British India, discusses the complex connections between imperialism and tropical medicine.[35] From West Bengal, the researches of Arabinda Samanta on malaria, Achintya Kumar Dutta on *kala-azar*, Suvankar Dey on tuberculosis, and Apalak Das on leprosy are significant. Sujata Mukherjee has addressed the issue of gender in colonial public health. Samanta's book on epidemics in colonial Bengal is a fruitful addition to the genre.[36] Most Indian scholars had referred to the European medical officers and the Indian Medical Service, but no analysis has been made with reference to a decline in the environmental situation of the colony. Sumit Guha has written a book on health and population in South Asia with a chapter on environmental sanitation in twentieth-century India.[37] The first reference to the environment in twentieth-century Calcutta is found a brief article by Dipankar Chakrabarti, published in Sukanta Chaudhuri's edited volume *Calcutta: The Living City*.[38] Arnold, in his book on toxic histories, analyses the histories of poison and pollution in India. He refers to environment in the context of pollution but that too in a general way that is applicable throughout India.[39] Recently, Nabaparna Ghosh has written an insightful account of the emerging discourses of health and hygiene within the *paras* or middle-class neighbourhoods of Calcutta. Ghosh analyses the competing claims on citizenship and leadership by upper-caste Hindu Bengalis. Hygiene, as she shows, made for hierarchies, and was related to the upper-caste Hindu concept of nation-making.[40] Her primary sources derive from the working of the Swarajya Party. Although such a rich and heterogeneous body of writings remain significant for any student of history, yet this historiography, developed largely in and for western European and north American contexts, can hardly be adopted for an environmental history of colonial Calcutta. Prajit Behari Mukherjee's research on the Bengali *daktars* and the context of nationalizing the body is significant but he also includes the grand narrative of imperialism and nation-making as the most relevant theroies in his discourse.[41] Sudipto Basu has argued that the so-called improvement projects carried out by the colonial state were based on the imaginings of the city administrators of the city space.[42] Recently, an edited volume by Suranjan Das and Achintya Kumar Dutta on the documentation of dreadful diseases in colonial Bengal is a remarkable addition to the history of public health in Bengal.[43]

However, most of these histories do not represent ecological responses based on a proper interpretation of the vernacular language space. As far as the history of Calcutta is concerned, scholars have rarely addressed the issues of pollution or environmental sanitation from the perspective of the geographical evolution of this city. There is perhaps a skepticism regarding the construction of a regional or city-based environmental history. One may also argue that environmental history is too young a sub-discipline to discuss the events of the nineteenth century. There is a confusion about what is crucial about environmental history or how to write it. Some answers are in this volume. Environmental history is a subject that can be global as well as local. Second, one can agree with scholars like Ramachandra Guha and Madhav Gadgil and regard the colonial period in India as an ecological watershed in history.[44] These scholars have informed us about the effects of the forest policy and Forest Acts, but the same exploitation occurred in the urban scenario as well. With improved method policy and tactics of resource extraction, the nineteenth century saw a new environmental crisis in India. Moreover, the empirical sources that we use for environmental history are not radically different from the archival materials of other branches of history. The basic tenets of environmental history should be sought within the structures of the modes of production, the stages of economic transformation, the hegemonic hierarchies of society culture and gender, and within the modernist narratives of the past. The only departure is that environmental history is much more holistic in approach; along with other sources it deals with histories of climate and other natural phenomenon, Environmental history is both micro-spatial and macro-spatial; along with the official archives it deals with all kinds of sources and addresses the responsive part of the hypothesis. It is generally nurtured in terms of giant strides in history.

The present volume investigates the extent of the success in developing the city of Calcutta and its impact on the environment. I begin my arguments in 1817, the year of the foundation of the Hindu College and the Lottery Committee. I end my search in 1923 to understand the response of the bhadralok and bhadramahila to the growth of science, planning, and development throughout the nineteenth and early twentieth century.[45] In the first chapter, the development of urban infrastructures will be discussed. To what extent those colonial efforts to make Calcutta a 'planned city' was compatible or incompatible with the developing notion of public health and sanitation, is the main thrust of the discussion here. In the second chapter the response of the educated middle -and upper-class Bengalis to the fast-changing surroundings has been dealt with. In the third chapter the voices of the bhadramahila or educated middle-class women have been analysed. In the concluding remarks I would like to argue that the relationship between urban development and environmental decay is ambiguous. The necessary evils of modern development left a huge impact on the surrounding environment. The urban social groups, aware of this nuanced process, participated in the same game consciously and to an extent the notion 'development' was prioritized over the environment.

Notes

1. For further details, see Mahua Sarkar, ed., 'Introduction' to *Environment and History: Recent Dialogues*, New Delhi: Kalpaz, 2007.

2. This kind of history-writing emerged mostly after the two world wars. See Samuel P. Hays, *Conservation and the Gospel of Efficiency: The Progressive Conservation Movement 1890–1920*, USA: University of Pittsburgh Press, 1959; repr., 1999. Also see Roderick Nash, *Wilderness and the American Mind*, Princeton: Yale University Press, 1973. In the USA, a generation of scholars came of age during the environmental movement of the sixties and the seventies. The publication of Rachel Carson's *Silent Spring* (1962), the passage of the Wilderness Act (1964) or the first Earth Day (1970) are seminal moments in the formation of their political consciousness.

3. Arun Bandyopadhyay, 'Towards an Understanding of the Environmental History of India', *Calcutta Historical Journal*, vol. XVI, no. 2, 1994, pp. 153–65.

4. Martin V. Melosi, 'The Place of the City in Environmental History', *Environmental Review*, vol. 111, 1979, p. 6.

5. Graeme Davison, 'The City as a Natural System: Theories of Urban Society in Early Nineteenth Century Britain', in *The Pursuit of Urban History*, ed. Detek Fraser and Anthony Sutcliffe, London: E. Arnold, 1983, p. 349.

6. Kristin Asdal, 'The Problematic Nature of Nature: The Post-Constructivist Challenge to Environmental History', *History and Theory*, vol. 42, no. 4, 2003, pp. 60–74.

7. Ibid.

8. Ibid.

9. Ibid.

10. P. Rainbow, ed., *The Foucault Reader*, New York: Pantheon Books, 1984, pp. 32–50. Also mentioned in Asdal, 'The Problematic Nature of Nature.'

11. Rainbow, *The Foucault Reader*.

12. Ibid.

13. Spenser W. Havlick, *The Urban Organism: The City's Natural Resources from an Environmental Perspective*, New York: Macmillan, 1974, p. 12.

14. David Harvey, *Social Justice and the City*, USA: Georgia University Press, 1973, p. 309.

15. Manuel Castells, *The City and the Grassroots: A Cross Cultural Theory of Urban Social Movements*, London: Hodder Arnold, 1983, p. 15.

16. Thomas R. Detwyler and Marvin G. Marcus, eds., *Urbanization and Environment: The Physical Geography of the City*, California: Duxbury Press, 1972, p. 10.

17. Melosi, 'The Place of the City in Environmental History', p. 7.

18. Ibid., p. 8.
19. Ian Douglas, 'Cities, an Environmental History', in *Environmental History and Global Change*, London: I.B. Tauris, 2013.
20. Lewis Mumford, *The City in History, Its Origins, Its Transformations and Its Prospects*, New York: MJF Books, 1961, p. 55.
21. Murari Ghosh, Alok Dutta, and Biswanath Ray, *Calcutta: A Case Study in Urban-Growth Dynamics*, Calcutta: Firma KLM, 1972, p. 8. Also see P.T. Nair, ed., *Job Charnock: The Founder of Calcutta: In Facts* and *Fiction: An Anthology: Calcutta*, Calcutta: Old Book Stall, 1977, pp. 14–15; Biren Roy, *Marshes to Metropolis: Calcutta 1481–1981*, Calcutta, National Council of Education, 1982, p. 16.
22. A.K. Ghosh, Introduction to *Urban Ecology: A Case Study of Calcutta*, Institute of Local and Urban Studies, Government of West Bengal, 1988.
23. Ibid.
24. See H. Beverly, *Report on the Census of Calcutta*, Calcutta: Bengal Secretariat Press, 1876, p. 41; H. James Rainey, *Historical and Topographical Sketch of Calcutta*, Calcutta: Englishman Press, 1876; *Calcutta Review*, vol. XVIII: Calcutta in the Older Times, its Localities, n.d.; H.E. Busteed, *Echoes from Old Calcutta*, New Delhi: Asian Educational Service, 1999; H.E.A. Cotton, *Calcutta Old and New: A Historical and Descriptive Handbook to the City*, Calcutta: W. Newman, 1907; Radharaman Mitra, *Kalikata Darpan*, parba 1, Calcutta: Subarnalekha, 1952; Bhabanicharan Bandyopadhyay, *Kalikata Kamalaya*, Calcutta: Ranjana Publishing House, 1951; Sivanath Sastri, *Ramtanu Lahiri o Tatkalin Brahmosamaj*, Calcutta: New Age Publishers, 1903; P. Thankappan Nair, *Calcutta in the 17th Century*, Calcutta: Firma KLM, 1986; P. Thankappan Nair, *Calcutta in the 18th*

Century, Calcutta: Firma KLM, 1984; P. Thankappan Nair, *Calcutta in the 19th Century: Company's Days*, Calcutta: Firma KLM, 1989; P. Thankappan Nair, *Calcutta : Origin of the Name*, Calcutta: Subarnarekha, 1985; P. Thankappan Nair, 'Civic and Public Services in Old Calcutta', in *Calcutta: the Living City*, vol I: The Past, ed. Sukanta Chaudhuri, New Delhi: Oxford University Press, 1990; S.N. Mukherjee, *Calcutta: Myths and Histories*, Calcutta: Subarnarekha, 1977; Asok Mitra, *Calcutta Diary*, Great Britain: Frank Cass and Co. Ltd, 1977; N.K. Bose, *Calcutta: 1964: A Social Survey*, Bombay: Lalvani, 1968.

25. Partho Datta, *Planning the City: Urbanization and Reform in Calcutta (1800–1940)*, New Delhi: Tulika Books, 2012; Debjani Bhattacharya, *Empire and Ecology in Bengal Delta: The Making of Calcutta*, UK: Cambridge University Press, 2018; Swati Chattopadhyay, *Representing Calcutta: Modernity, Nationalism and Colonial Uncanny*, UK: Psychology Press, 2005.

26. Sumanta Banerjee, *Memoirs of Roads: Calcutta from Colonial Urbanization to Global Modernizaton*, New Delhi: Oxford University Press, 2016.

27. Anindita Ghosh, *Claiming the City: Protest, Crime and Scandals in Colonial Calcutta, c. 1860–1920*, New Delhi: Oxford University Press, 2016.

28. Anthony D. King, *Colonial Urban Development: Culture, Social Power and Environment*, London: Routledge, 1976, p. 39.

29. Dipesh Chakrabarty, 'In Defense of "Provincializing Europe": A Response to Carola Dietze', *History and Theory*, vol. 47, no. 1, 2008, p. 86.

30. Deepak Kumar, *Science and the Raj: A Study of the British India*, New Delhi: Oxford University Press, 2006; Mark Harrison, *Climate and Constitutions: Health, Race, Environment and British Imperialism*

in India, 1600–1850, New Delhi: Oxford University Press, 1999.

31. Mark Harrison, *Public Health in British India: Anglo-Indian Preventive Medicine, 1859–1914*, Cambridge: Cambridge University Press, 1994.

32. David Arnold, *Colonizing the Body: State Medicine and Epidemic Disease in Nineteenth Century India*, Berkeley: University of California Press, 1993; Harrison, *Climates and Constitutions*; Roger Jeffery, *The Politics of Health in India*, Berkeley: University of California Press, 1998; Kumar, *Science and the Raj*; Radhika Ramasubban, *Public Health and Medical Research in India: Their Origins and Development under the Impact of British Colonial Policy*, Stockholm: SAREC, 1982; Poonam Bala, *Imperialism and Medicine in Bengal: A Socio-Historical Perspective*, New Delhi: Sage, 1991.

33. Kabita Ray, *History of Public Health: Colonial Bengal (1921–1947)*, Calcutta: K.P. Bagchi and Co., 1998.

34. Srirupa Prasad, *Cultural Politics of Hygiene in India (1890–1940)*, UK: Palgrave Macmillan, 2015, pp. 1–22.

35. Pratik Chakrabarti, *Bacteriology in British India: Laboratory Medicine and the Tropics*, UK: Boydell and Brewer, 2013.

36. Arabinda Samanta, *Living with Epidemics in Colonial Bengal*, New Delhi: Manohar, 2017; Chittabrata Palit and Achintya Kumar Dutta, eds., *The History of Medicine in India: The Medical Encounter*, New Delhi: Kalpaz, 2005. For further details see Suvankar Dey, 'The Silent Killer: Tuberculosis in Colonial and Post-Colonial Bengal (1911–1962)', unpublished PhD dissertation, Kolkata, Jadavpur University, 2019, and Apalak Das, 'Leprosy in Bengal, c. 1873–1956', unpublished PhD dissertation, Kolkata, Jadavpur University, 2021.

37. Sumit Guha, *Health and Population in South Asia: From Earliest Times to the Present*, Ranikhet: Permanent Black, 2010, p. 118.
38. Dipankar Chakrabarti, 'Calcutta's Environment', in *Calcutta the Living City*, vol II: The Present and Future, ed. Sukanta Chaudhuri, New Delhi: Oxford University Press, 1990, pp. 181–9.
39. David Arnold, *Toxic Histories: Poison and Pollution in Modern India*, UK: Cambridge University Press, 2016.
40. Nabaparna Ghosh, *A Hygienic City-Nation: Space, Community and Everyday Life in Colonial Calcutta*, UK: Cambridge University Press, 2016.
41. Prajit Bihari Mukharji, *Nationalizing the Body: The Medical Market and Daktari Medicine*, Kolkata: Anthem Press, 2009.
42. Sudipto Basu, 'Spatial Imagination and Development in Colonial Calcutta, c. 1850–1900', *History and Sociology of South Asia*, vol. 10, no. 1, 2015, p. 36.
43. Suranjan Das and Achinyta Kumar Dutta, eds., *Dreadful Diseases in Colonial Bengal: Cholera, Malaria and Smallpox*, New Delhi: Primus Books, 2021.
44. Madhav Gadgil and Ramachandra Guha, eds., *This Fissured Land: An Ecological History of India*, Berkeley: University of California Press, 1993; Ramachandra Guha, *The Unquiet Woods: Ecological Change and Peasant Resistance in the Himalaya*, Berkley: University of California Press, 2000.
45. For our current purpose, I use categories such as bhadralok and 'Bengali upper-caste Hindu elites' more or less interchangeably.

1

Scientific Infrastructure and Urban Development in Calcutta

Anthropological and morphological connotations of human and natural existence have converged in the best possible way within the urban scenario. The present discussion on the urban development and scientific infrastructure will focus on the inner nuances of this encounter. The conceptualization of urban space as a broad sphere for the development of socio-ecological relationships is an emerging and much-debated area of study. Historians are often reluctant to examine 'human development and progresses' in the context of environmental history. The environment is not simply rural and aesthetic; it also encompasses the crowded, the polluted, and the urban. Because of its interdisciplinary nature and unique focus on humans and natural systems, the term 'urban ecology' has been used to describe the study of humans in cities, of nature in cities, and of the coupled relationships between humans and nature.[1]

There were divisions within the city of Calcutta like the white town, the black town, and the intermediate zones, exhibiting a hierarchy of urban improvement on the basis of caste, class, and racial differentiation which affected the environmental balance of the place. The developmental works were mainly initiated in the white town by colonial authorities, whereas the black town was left in the hands of the zamindars who did not bother about improving the sanitary condition of the markets and the overall health of the city.[2] Thus, from the beginning, Calcutta had developed as a city of palaces and a city of slums. With the development of science, scientific institutions, and teaching institutions, no comprehensive and consistent measure for the improvement of public health was undertaken and there was a gradual yet chaotic awareness of public health and pollution in nineteenth-century Calcutta. This idea awareness emerged through the expertise of some early colonial officers, surveyors, and scientists.[3] The 'native people', who were eager to receive Western knowledge, were supported by the colonial government, which granted money for the promotion of Western education. By the late eighteenth and early nineteenth centuries, the civil and military officers and engineers of the East India Company and the Jesuit missionaries brought in knowledge of geography, astronomy, and geology in India. The Asiatic Society, founded in Calcutta in 1784, nurtured the growth of European science through the publication of scientific articles and journals. It also encouraged antiquarian research on ancient Indian science. The 'native people' were actively involved in the foundation of Hindu College, formally opened on 20 January 1817, providing courses on grammer, writing, history, geography, astronomy, mathematics, and English literature. The Serampore College, founded on 15 August 1818 by William Carey, J. Marshman, and W. Ward, propagated European science through its educational programme.[4] The Bengali bhadralok were also helped by the foundation of Medical College in 1835, which offered a space for studies in modern Western medicine and allopathic treatment.

From the seventeenth century, hospitals and dispensaries for European sailors, soldiers, and civilians were established to decrease death rates. These places became sites of innovations of Western medicines, morbid anatomy, and therapeutics.[5] I must refer to a few British scientists and pathologists who were working in the city, such as Robert Koch (1843–1910), Ronald Ross (1857–1932), and Waldemar Haffkin (1860–1930). They were scientific explorers who studied colonies of microbes under a microscope. The 'institution' was fashioned in a way that allowed Thomas Babington Macaulay and William Bentinck to design the future of education in India. The same institution saw the development of a 'scientific temper' in the colony.[6] The importation of knowledge from metropolis to periphery was never a linear process. It moulded both participants, as the situation in the colonies was also ripe for the reception of that knowledge. The people of Calcutta, including the Europeans and middle-class Bengalis, had attained a kind of scientific cognition in the nineteenth century. Noted personalities like Rammohun Roy, the Derozians and various associations such as the Society for the Acquisition of General Knowledge (SAGK) and the bilingual journal like *Gnanayneshwan*, were all thinking in terms of advancement of scientific knowledge and development of knowledge systems. The University of Calcutta (1858) from the very beginning tried to incorporate natural and physical sciences in its courses but the dogmatism prevailing during that time hindered its growth.[7] The incorporation of proper scientific knowledge in the undergraduate courses, a much-debated issue in the senate (the university's governing body), also faced a lack of appropriate teaching faculty. Indeed, the process of imparting scientific knowledge through classrooms had a deep impact on society. But on the other hand, the newly introduced scientific knowledge was compatible with Indian minds. Treatment procedures always had establish compatibility with the needs of the patient, which showed a deliberate effort on the part of the colonial masters to adapt to their contemporary situation. During the 1860s there were conscious efforts to initiate a proper and efficient system of instruction in natural science in the curriculum of Calcutta University.[7] Most of the funds for the development of the faculty of science came from the contributions of Indians to the university.[8] In this context the donations made by Taraknath Palit and the efforts of vice-chancellors like Sir Ashutosh Mukherjee are worth mentioning. Thus, nineteenth and early twentieth century Calcutta offered a new picture on the scientific temper that was previously missing.

The development of science was not backed by the growth of public health in Calcutta. The ideology of scientism emerged while the city remained unclean. In the year 1891, much after than the establishment of Calcutta Medical College and Calcutta University,

Pulin Chandra Sanyal wrote in *Chikitsa Sammilani* that in spite of serious efforts to improve the health of the city, the condition of the land surrounding the city remained as unhygienic as it was previously. In the rainy season, one could not live in the ground floor of houses in Calcutta and floors became muddy.[9] This reference shows how science was developing in an unclean city.

The notion of tropical medicine, exclusive to the Indian subcontinent, had considerably delayed the acceptance of the germ theory of disease in British India. Still, one can argue that with colonial help, inspiration, and research the idea of looking at diseases in Calcutta from the perspective of miasma theory, relating to climatic disorder, gradually transformed into a scientific theory of disease. The idea that diseases could be fought with the help of medicines was encouraged by scholars like Francis Macnamara, who was a professor of chemistry at Calcutta Medical College, and Sir Leonard Rogers who was a believer in the institutionalization of medical research.[10] Rogers was responsible for the foundation of the Calcutta School of Tropical Medicine. Because of the constant encouragement given to research and development of the medical world, the All India Institute of Hygiene and Public Health was established in Calcutta in 1932. Unfortunately, from the perspective of the history of epidemics and pandemics, public health remained limited to the compilation of rather inaccurate statistics and obviously there was a haphazard growth of medical knowledge in the city. Medico journals published from the city referred to indigenous and Western methods of treatment in the same volumes, often declaring the indigenous methods as the better of the two. For instance, Jyotindranath Mukhopadhyay in *Swasthya Samachar* (1912) compared the Western method of using soap with the indigenous method of using oil, stating that the latter was better for maintaining good health in tropical countries.[11] At the same time, a general trend emerged that saw the development of a city in the colonial scenario as parasitic. This kind of argument should address the variations and inner complications in urban development. The growth of Calcutta, Bombay, and Delhi during the colonial period cannot be treated in one trajectory as these cities did not exhibit a similar kind of urban ecology. Rather, it can be argued that a colonial city like Calcutta was not solely parasitic as its rural roots were silently persistent throughout the period of development of the city. The link between the rural and the urban was always there as the growth of Calcutta was not necessarily connected with the growth of industrialization. During the nineteenth century, there was an influx of people from rural areas and at the same time there was a growing concern towards modern concepts of public health. S.W. Goode, Deputy Commissioner of the Calcutta Corporation, has given the following estimate of population of Calcutta between 1800 and 1911, depicted in Plate 1.

It is difficult to determine if the urban population growth of Calcutta in the nineteenth and in the first half of the twentieth centuries occurred in response to the real economic need for large urban concentrations—i.e. due to greater employment opportunities and brighter income prospects from new industrial developments

        1800. Police Commissioners' estimate .   500,000
        1802. Chief Magistrate's   "   .   600,000
        1814. Sir E. Hyde's   "   .   700,000
        1815. East India Gazetteer   "   .   500,000
        1821. Assessor's   "   .   230,502
        1831. Captain Steel's   "   .   411,000
        1837. Captain Birch's   "   .   230,000
        1840. Simms'   "   .   361,000
        1850. Chief Magistrate's   "   .   413,000

POPULATION FROM CENSUS OF 1872 TO CENSUS OF 1911

Town.	1872.	1881.	1891.	1901.	1911.
Wards.					
1. Shampooker	28,848	28,511	36,885	46,887	53,036
2. Koomartooly	34,024	25,682	26,614	30,155	33,073
3. Burtolla	29,923	28,935	36,431	50,216	54,610
4. Sookea's Street	25,036	24,405	34,828	42,034	48,112
5. Jorabagan	39,076	36,318	39,180	49,069	52,114
6. Jorasanko	36,029	32,824	41,657	52,988	59,541
7. Burrabazar	23,503	20,769	20,646	31,574	30,495
8. Colootolla	50,805	47,323	50,781	63,170	57,094
9. Moocheepara	43,639	43,581	49,472	64,116	63,362
10. Bowbazar	23,543	21,627	22,668	27,052	25,014
11. Paddapukker	20,486	20,516	20,761	28,060	29,966
12. Waterloo Street	5,704	5,785	5,932	6,302	6,284
13. Fenwick Bazar	26,787	25,898	28,366	31,208	28,436
14. Taltolla	27,112	26,063	29,207	32,237	32,112
15. Collinga	12,773	11,840	13,218	16,780	11,385
16. Park Street	4,566	4,968	4,620	6,110	5,294
17. Bamun Bustee	6,568	6,125	4,598	5,454	3,125
18. Hastings	5,153	5,115	4,820	5,919	5,550
19. Entally	27,271	26,929	33,892	38,626	45,072
20. Beniapooker	20,289	18,895	23,020	28,202	37,881
21. Ballygunge and Tollygunge.	23,329	20,423	22,831	27,207	39,952
22. Bhowanipur.	37,118	38,002	42,591	49,641	54,569
23. Alipore	19,419	13,438	14,804	17,718	19,749
24. Ekbalpur	18,074	15,869	15,340	21,608	21,869
25. Watgunj	23,030	27,920	26,833	37,918	43,806
Outside Municipal Area.					
Inside Fort	...	2,942	3,468	2,893	4,411
Outside Fort	...	397	151	437	
Port	6,660	28,200	26,589	29,768	26,890
Canals	11,761	3,007	2,102	4,447	3,265
Total	633,009	612,307	682,305	847,796	896,067

Plate 1: Estimate of Calcutta's population, 1800–1911

Source: S.W. Goode, *Municipal Calcutta: Its Constitutions in their Origin and Growth*, Edinburgh: The Corporation of Calcutta, T & A Constable, 1916, p. 361.

in the city—or due to factors arising out of the steadily deteriorating situation in the villages. I have already mentioned how old village communities and the bases of rural social organizations were disrupted by the 'investment' and 'land-revenue' policies of the East India Company. By highlighting both issues of development and decay together, I argue that in the long run eco-degradation and decline of public health had been undermining the quality of life from the beginning of colonial rule. Throughout the nineteenth and twentieth centuries the British made conscious efforts towards establishing a sense of cleanliness by setting up dispensaries and hospitals, implementing vaccinations and sanitary schemes relating to water supply, drainage, and conservancy as shown by the studies of Mark Harrison and many other scholars.[12]

The word 'purity' is spatial, individual, public as well as socially constructed. Thus, it manifold implications. According to Webster's Dictionary, to 'pollute' means 'to make physically impure' or 'unclean' or 'to contaminate the environment especially with man-made waste'. The term is not related only to the modern urban scenario; this connotation was prevalent since premodern times. In India, the word was used in wider social and cultural contexts. It can be argued that the theory of purity or pollution arising from birth was inherent in the varna system which denied access to social prestige and power to so-called impure castes through non-polluting occupations. The principle emerged mainly due to the widening of social distance between seemingly dominant and subservient communities. This notion of pollution had also influenced the Islamic society of Bengal from the thirteenth to sixteenth centuries. Kabikankan Mukundaram Chakrabarti, in his *Chandimangal*, mentions fifteen Muslim jatis in a list of communities living in a typical Bengali city during the time he was writing. Of these people, the so-called 'impure' groups like scavengers, gravediggers, and sweepers were practically living as Untouchables. Naturally, these notions of ritual purity created artificial divisions on the basis of power and thereby made society hierarchical, differentiated and polluted in itself. Apart from this unscientific idea of physical pollution regarding birth or occupation, the scientific or eco-friendly attitude towards pollution was also found in ancient texts like the *Charakasamhita*. There, all forms of environmental pollution were termed as *bikriti*, and pollution from sound and odour, etc., were specified. People were requested to maintain cleanliness in open masses of land and water, and if they disobeyed, serious punishments were to be meted out. While these ideas of purity/pollution did not change drastically in the medieval times, they received a new dimension with the advent of Western conceptions of public health and new ideas about diseases. These public health measures of environmental sanitation could not create islands of purity in India because the basic intention of these efforts was to protect the army and colonial administrators. The colonizers who were trying to improve the health scenario of the city were ignorant of the etiology of indigenous diseases. Obviously, this issue of public health was related to the poetics of colonial finance as well. The initiatives taken in the periphery were always influenced by changes in the metropole. Roy Porter has argued that none of the early sanitarians in England were doctors.[13] The Chadwick Report of 1842 shows that there was an outbreak of diseases in England which was connected with the lack of the facilities; after that, proper finances were dispensed to improve the sanitary condition of the people.[14] This was never done in the same scale in a colonial city like Calcutta. There was a striking similarity of this report with J.R. Martin's *Medical Topography* of 1837, which highlighted the sanitary conditions of early Calcutta. In the report, Martin repeatedly complains about the city's dirty, narrow, unpaved roads.[15] However, colonial considerations to improve the space of Calcutta began with the question of legalizing public health. The Contagious Diseases Act of 1864 was passed to keep pace with the health needs of the army. Reports from government offices show that with colonialism, there were major developments in the structure of public health and the emergence of different kinds of professions and institutions for that purpose. But the entire scheme remains superficial as there was greater concern for finance and the colonial government avoided any measures that would provoke acute hostility among the common people.

The city of Calcutta began as a miasmatic land; along with the planning of new urban spaces, the psychological fear of contamination also prevailed there. The earliest date of the establishment of 'pauper hospitals' (i.e. hospitals for the poor) can be traced back to 1789. These were destined to be asylums and refuges for the destitute. This effort was not temporary as is evident from Act XI of 1867, which enabled justices of peace to levy a police tax and to use municipal funds to support the pauper hospitals.[16]

Gradually, the administration of pauper hospitals were taken up directly by the colonial government and the allocation of funds was raised from Rs.35,000 in 1894 to Rs.41,000 in 1909 by the corporation.[17] The management of the paupers was crucial for the developing urban character of the city. Not only native paupers but also Europeans used to take refuge in these hospitals. Later, they took in smallpox patients as well. In 1848–50 and 1856–8 there was a severe outbreak of smallpox, but vaccination was rejected by a large part of the community. As a consequence, the vaccination process was remodelled and strengthened, which included the assistance of a host of vaccinators under the immediate supervision of a head vaccinator. According to the annual report of the Sanitary Commissioner during the year 1895–6, the supervising staff in Bengal consisted of 3 deputy sanitary commissioners, 48 civil surgeons, 211 native superintendents and 13 head vaccinators.[18] As the Minute of Wellesley argued for a comprehensive urban scenario connecting the cityscape with public health, the later efforts on the part of the government can be analysed through this perspective. In the proceedings of the Municipal Department (Sanitation), January 1911, the expansion of the office of the Sanitary Commissioner was recorded. Three clerks at Rs.30 a month were appointed to assist in the compilation of statistics for the annual sanitary and vaccination reports.[19] Goode, in his book, mentioned various aspects of public health that were grabbing the attention of the colonial rulers. Inspection of food, disposal of dead bodies, supply of dairy products, establishment of hospitals, and vaccination procedures, were all attached to the general picture of the public health of nineteenth- and twentieth-century Calcutta. The colonial government's need for these initiatives is not the main point of argument. Any socio-political or cultural growth under the colonial government was bound to be restrained by many prejudices and imaginations. But the repercussion of those initiatives was felt throughout the indigenous society, which will be discussed in detail in the following section of this chapter.

For many decades, modern history has been seen as a saga of either 'European benevolence' or of the cruel savages of colonialism. Recently, an earnest need has arisen to see the process beyond the one-dimensional core-periphery lens. An urge to understand the ecological hybridity of a complex city like Calcutta has emerged. The foundation of the Lottery Committee or Town Improvement Committee in 1817 was the first significant step towards regularizing the urban environment in early nineteenth-century Calcutta. As the nature of colonial rule during this time was solely dependent on military power, the need for a compatible mode of transportation led to the establishment of the Lottery Committee. In his famous Minute of 1803, Lord Wellesley foresighted this committee through which colonial masters tended to collect public funds for the development of the cityscape. The final culmination of these improvement plans can be seen in the formation of the Calcutta Improvement Trust (CIT) in 1911. The framework for the present study thus has been guided by the continuum of the improvement efforts of the colonial masters and its impact on the urban environment.

Urbanization is a complex process of human development. On the one hand it diversifies people and their activities, encourages innovation, and creates new opportunities. On the other hand, urbanization leads human civilization to the problem of massive environmental degradation. It is generally believed that the question of urban development can never be addressed without reference to urban disasters. This is particularly true of colonial Calcutta. I have not discussed natural disasters like cyclones and storms in this volume.[20] It is the history of urban ecology of Calcutta that was gradually losing its sustainability in spite of the so-called 'growth' in the colonial period. However, this process started much earlier. Debjani Bhattacharya has shown that, from the eighteenth century, human intervention managed and radically transformed the movements of land and water in and around Calcutta.[21] With the transfer of capital from Dhaka to Murshidabad and finally to Calcutta, the latter gained the attention of the colonial masters; this is when the environmental disasters began. Calcutta did not have the rich urban heritage of a Dhaka or a Murshidabad. While the heritage of the latter two cities can be traced to the medieval period, Calcutta at that time was a trading mart with rural settlements. Rila Mukherjee stated that Bengal, with Calcutta as the capital, had 'an unparalleled diversity of trade goods, a low cost of living, a weak merchant class and cheap commodity prices' and in spite of its unhealthy climate and humidity.[22] The cluster of Govindapur, Sutanuti, and Kolikata offered a vast space for expansion and development. But this scenario, as far as the geography and the climate were concerned, was not fit for sustainable growth. The East India Company's records show how the early officers lamented about the climate and how the famous 'Calcutta fever', which was later discovered to be 'malaria' or 'influenza', was a regular occurrence in the new city.[23] Fever was natural in Calcutta as it was a city with a moist, miasmatic climate; it was alien to the Europeans and was not considered fit for habitation. However, the situation improved with the gradual development of medical research in Calcutta. Institutional structures like the Medical College and other hospitals as well as basic infrastructures like roads, streets, and bridges were also built during this. In the period between 1817 and 1836, the Lottery Committee gave Calcutta its first taste of town planning and improvement. The finest example of this was the creation of a number of roads like Central Road, Wood Street, Wellesley Street, Wellington Street, College Street, and Cornwallis Street.[24] Three aspects were initiated at the same time: (a) massive acquisition of land for semi-public use; (b) improvements made for the development of British trade in Calcutta; and (c) filling up of canals and waterbodies for a mass transportation corridor. At the same time, many legal cases were being filed in the newly established Calcutta High Court (Act of 1861), by the Calcutta bhadralok against land acquisition by the government. One such case was filed by Manick Chand Mahata on 16 February 1921 against the government acquisition of the building he lived in for widening the street. In the judgement, the court decided that the proper cost of the building, worth Rs.70,000 and the market value of which was Rs. 2,50,000 should be paid off by the corporation and the CIT. But this case was an exception to the general rule of land acquisition at a much lower cost than the actual value.[25]

The heyday for retailers and tradesmen was the 1860s and 1870s when free trade was maximized and improvements in transportation and communications allowed profitable expansion of business.[26] This expansion was expressed in the growth of British business farms in Calcutta. Andrew Yule in tea, jute, and coal; McLeod Russell in tea; Balmer Lawrie in engineering and coal; Octavius Steel in tea, coal, railways, and limestone; Williamson Magor in tea and inland navigation; and Macneill and Barry in tea and jute were examples of entrants into the business world of Calcutta who did not originate in Asian trade.[27] A large number of tanks and pools were filled up under hygienic conditions for construction purposes. Creek Row was constructed by filling up an old creek flowing eastward. In this period, members of the Tagore family referred to their residential pond in Jorasanko and Kshitidranath Tagore mentioned another pond in Singhabagan that were filled up with rubbish by the municipalities.[28] In 1914, the CIT started a project to link Beadon Street to Dharmatolla Street, which required the removal of some 'insanitary slum areas' and the destructions of old buildings situated in narrow, winding lanes. This scheme also helped relieve traffic congestions in Chitpore Road and Cornwallis Street.[29] Thus, the disappearance of the slums and the construction of varied architectural designs were taking place side by side during this period, which aimed at solving the traffic problem in Calcutta. Narayani Gupta refers to the surveys of E.P.

Richards in Calcutta (1914) and informs us that he was shocked to find a small, planned area separated by a circular road that acted as a dividing boundary, enclosing densely packed and street-less habitations. She argues that this pattern was a typical feature of a town dominated by an alien power.[30] Marshall Berman has aptly revealed the true nature of urban ecology in the nineteenth and twentieth centuries. According to him, during the nineteenth century, urban planning took place in order to incorporate the dynamism that materialized due to confrontation with a new space. During the twentieth century, these efforts of reconciliation had failed due to improper execution.[31] Since 'improvement trusts' were very popular in nineteenth-century Britain, these were set up in India as well; first in Bombay in 1898 and then in Calcutta in 1911. After dealing with various reports and proceedings of the CIT and the Corporation it is now very clear that the term 'town-planning' was occasionally used in a general way and sometimes in a very specific way. Town-planning implied intervention by colonial officials in the guise of development and management to meet the demands of the contemporary situation. Such an intervention had long-lasting environmental repercussions, such as alterations in the land surface, overuse of water supply, overcrowding, growing stagnation of garbage, dust, smoke, increasing pollution, and degradation of public health. The link between coercive institutions like the court and the police and the promotion of Calcutta as a cityscape explains the complications of colonial hegemony. Dipesh Chakrabarty speaks of certain ideas of beauty related to the management of public space and interests.[32] This order of aesthetics cannot be separated from the ideals of public health and hygiene. He refers to Wellesley's Minute of 1803 in support of his argument:

In those quarters of the town occupied principally by the native inhabitants, the houses have been built without order or regularity, and the streets and lanes have been formed without attention to the health, convenience or safety of the inhabitants.... The appearance and beauty of the town are inseparably connected with the health, safety and convenience of the inhabitants, and every improvement ... will tend to ameliorate the climate and to promote and secure ... a just and salutary system of police.[33]

Similar expressions are found in European writings throughout the nineteenth century. As far as the Indian situation was concerned, urbanization and pollution went hand in hand from the beginning of colonial rule. During the nineteenth century, the Lottery Committee was abolished and the Fever Hospital Committee (1836) and the Municipal Improvement Committee emerged from the intensive inquiry on the conditions and needs of municipal Calcutta. The principle that was firmly established after this enquiry was that any adequate scheme of improvement must be based on a comprehensive drainage system. The municipal authorities in the early colonial days were mainly concerned with cleansing the streets and proper drainage systems. The Municipal Improvement Committee (1809) and the Lottery Committee (1817) subsequently executed many works of public utility.[34] But all these schemes needed a secure and continuous flow of funds that was a serious problem for the colony.

It seemed inconceivable to comprehend this financial crisis regarding development in the age of 'drain of wealth'. The main sources of funds for development, thus, were the house tax and excise duties.[35] In 1836, the Lottery Committee succumbed to public opinion in England which condemned the method of raising money in this way for municipal purposes. Ultimately the Bengal Municipal Act of 1848 empowered the Municipal Improvement Committee to collect revenue for sanitary works.[36] Under the Calcutta Municipal Act of 1863, the municipal government imposed a water rate and the house tax was raised to a maximum of 10 per cent. In 1864, the first health officer of Calcutta was appointed, his purpose being the supervision of surface conservancy and condition of roads. The inspectors of markets acted as his general assistants. Six registrars of births and deaths were also appointed. The Calcutta Corporation was further reconstituted by the Municipal Acts of 1876 and definite sanitary obligations were imposed by the Calcutta Municipal Act of 1923.[37] The government officers were mandated to construct toilets in the slums of Calcutta; however, the toilet habits of the people could not be changed so easily. Thus, throughout the nineteenth century there were discussions and planning in official circles about the development of the health scenario of Calcutta.[38] In spite of colonial constructions, Calcutta—physically, socially and culturally—for the indigenous people remained mostly a rural settlement. Throughout the nineteenth century the city had large paddy lands, mud roads, water bodies and thatched mud huts. Geographically and culturally, it retained its rural-urban continuity in an otherwise urban scenario.[39] The Mayors Court, the Privy Council, the Lottery Committee and the various town-planning and municipal bodies in the nineteenth century were part of the process of acquiring this watery, swampy land and turning it into a concrete jungle. All these efforts culminated in Calcutta Improvement Act of 1911 which ultimately came into force on 2 January 1912. Cecil Henry Bompas, the first Chairman of the CIT, began his account with a description of the plague of 1896 which became an epidemic between 1900 and 1905. In 1896, a Medical Commission inquired into local conditions and its revelations led to the establishment of the Calcutta Building Commission in 1897. This commission drew attention to the need for controlling the growth of the town and recommended the creation of an improvement trust, like the Bombay Improvement Trust that had been established in 1898.[40] In the opinion of Partho Datta, the CIT was controlled by European bureaucrats and Indians had only a token presence in the organization. In land acquisition and the politics around it, the CIT had the full support of the colonial state and for this reason it became the major driving force behind the restructuring of the city.[41] But in Calcutta, the situation was not as favourable as Bombay, as in the former city there was no land at the disposal of the government due to Permanent Settlement. Primarily, the imperial government was not ready to finance local improvements with imperial revenue. But later revenues from five various sources were placed at the disposal of the CIT and it was ultimately created, 'to make provision for the improvement and expansion of Calcutta by opening up congested areas, laying out and altering streets, providing open spaces for purposes of ventilation or recreation, and for re-housing persons of the poorer and working classes displaced by the operations of the Trust'.[42]

Henry Lefebvre, in his book *The Production of Space* argued that the urban space was produced in order to achieve certain abstract purposes, including political and economic domination by the state. He further argued that such a space was highly political in nature and its aim was to create a sense of homogeneity that would iron out all differing perspectives like a bulldozer. Thus, the purpose of city planning was the production of a political space with the view of absolute domination by the state. The material purpose of the abstract space was that it would be understood and worked out in terms of its exchange value and, therefore, a process of commodification of the urban space began to take place.[43] In the case of the CIT, this notion of commodification of urban spaces can be understood from the perspective of environmental decay. The Annual Report on the Operations of the Calcutta Improvement Trust for the year 1921–2 includes the receipts from the duty on the transfer of property during 1920–1; these indicate that the land boom of the previous three years had reached its height in March 1920 and the municipal contribution amounted to Rs.11,12,833 against Rs.10,32,698 from the previous year. This amount steadily increased from Rs.7,37,000—the first annual contribution made to the CIT in 1912–13.[44] At the beginning of 1922, there were 376 undemolished buildings in the possession of the CIT. In the course of that year it obtained possession of 291 more buildings in different schemes.[45] These statistics pointed to the increasing importance of the CIT in the sphere of town planning. Not only was the transfer of property or land acquisition crucial to the work of the CIT, so was the re-housing of people. At a meeting on 2 September 1918, a sub-committee was appointed to submit definite proposals regarding provisions that could be made re-house poorer persons and working classes as well as to reinstate bhadralok houseowners.[46] Plots in Paikpara and Manicktala were available for the purpose of re-housing, as were houses built in Kerbala Tank Lane.[47]

As Calcutta was the second metropolitan city of the British Empire, it could not escape the impact of the First World War. C.H. Bompas in his report elaborately discussed the difficulties faced by the CIT during this time. The first issue was that engineering materials such as iron pipes and cement became increasingly expensive, which compelled the CIT to cut down large schemes regarding the displacement of the population.[48] When the war ended the increase in the cost of engineering works was made permanent which meant that the CIT schemes had to be modified. The price of land also increased during this period; there was a property boom in Calcutta followed by a slump. Speculators who bought land during the boom faced huge losses and further buying of land was discouraged. The assets of the CIT were frozen. But Bompas was hopeful that the phase would pass soon.[49] H.V. Lanchester, in his review of Richards' report made an argument that the 'house famine' in Calcutta was likely to become more acute merely through the destruction of slums for the purpose of building new main roads.[50] The slum area was decreasing as the colonial government concentrated on the beautification and commercialization of the city.[51] With the growth of the city, the character of the CIT also changed from a land developer to a so-called promoter of the developing city. Various CIT schemes were initiated. For example, in a special meeting of the board held on 23 February 1935 regarding the budget estimation of the Improvement Trust Scheme (XVI), the widening of Diamond Harbour was brought up. The colonial government followed every step previously taken by such trusts in Britain and Bombay. Its policy towards slum areas was also affected by such ideals. They assumed that the unhealthy, congested slum areas were the breeding ground of epidemics. As a result, the demolition of these areas was the only option to create a healthy environment in the city. Bompas made a comparison between England and India on the issue of re-housing. In England it was easy to provide homes for every family but in India only those who could avail re-housing were given aid.[52] As rehousing was provided only to the highest bidders (who were the bhadralok), this ended in the large-scale displacement of the poor masses. Thus, it seemed that there was a vicious cycle of making and unmaking the environment of the city under colonial rule. In the case of the working of the CIT, England had set some precedence but that did not mean that the former's efforts were half-hearted.

It can be argued that a system of knowledge inspires the representation of spaces, which in turn plays an important role in social practice. That continuous presence of modern knowledge was evident in the workings of the CIT in twentieth-century Calcutta. Sumanta Banerjee, in his *Memoirs of Roads*, explains the political economy of the road-building process, which ensured the smooth execution of trading and military works and also had a huge impact on human habitations. The transport system and the building of houses were all affected by the construction of roads.[53] In the case of Calcutta, Richards mentioned in his report that there was no relation between street planning in the city proper and in the suburbs.[54] Since 1888, the Calcutta Corporation had paid attention to street building and, gradually, roads like Lansdowne Road, Harish Mukherjee Road, and Hazra Road came into existence. Richards also argued that the narrow lanes in Calcutta were the main routes for traffic.

The first motor car was seen on the streets of Calcutta in 1896. Various types of cars, designed and made by leading automobile manufacturers across the world were found in Calcutta in those days. Taxis would run across the entire city, even to peripheral regions like Dum Dum, Barrackpore, and Budge Budge.[55] The standardized fare was 8 annas per mile. After the horse-driven trams, the first motorized bus started to operate in Calcutta in 1922. A very important event in this regard was the launching of public buses by the Walford Company. Within a short span of time, the Company became the major bus operator in Calcutta, even introducing double-decker buses to the city. The main bus depot was located near Lalbazar, towards the east of Bentinck Street. The Automobile Association of Bengal was established in Calcutta on 28 August 1904.[56] Cars and buses began to consume a lot of energy before they ever made it to the open road. Automotive production had a giant carbon footprint because materials like steel, rubber, glass, plastics, paints, and many other were necessary for the creation of every new automotive. Similarly, the end of a car's life did not mark the end of its environmental impact. The dumping of plastics, toxic battery acids, junkyard pile-ups, steel frames and other products had an adverse effect on the environment. Production, recycling, and disposal costs to the environment were difficult to quantify and largely beyond the control of most consumers. It was also true that most of an automobile's environmental impact, perhaps 80 to 90 per cent, was due to fuel consumption and emissions of air pollution and greenhouse gases. Unfortunately, the level of this impact was not under the control of the driver. Petroleum products raised environmental red flags even before they were burnt. Extracting them from the earth was an energy-intensive process that could damage local ecosystems. Shipping fuel consumed a lot of energy and created occasional environmental disasters such as oil spills. The main concern in Calcutta was not the increasing traffic but the general health of the city and the housing concern in which streets, bridges, and canals had an important role to play. In Section 39 of the Bengal Act no. V of 1911, it has been stated that streets could be constructed for the purpose of providing building sites, remedying defective ventilation, providing facilities for traffic, *or affording better facilities for conservancy* (italics mine).[57] However, such construction projects were never undertaken with conservancy in mind. The annual report of the CIT for 1921–2 mentioned the construction of three very important bridges—

Dum Dum Bridge, Khidderpore Bridge, and Howrah Bridge. The responsibility of the reconstruction of the Khidderpore Bridge over Tolly's Nullah was taken over jointly by the CIT, the Calcutta Corporation, and the Irrigation Department. These were developmental works undertaken by the CIT that did not leave any sphere of urban life untouched.[58] The Report does not refer to any policy of conservancy, it only dealt with constructions, which bolstered the urban character of the city.

Health and sanitation are crucial parts of the urbanization process. Issues of land acquisition, re-housing, improvement of roads, etc., are deeply entrenched within the issue of public health and sanitation. In 1911, the *Proceedings* of the Lieutenant-Governor of Bengal (Municipal Branch) mentioned that it was the primary duty of the CIT to enquire into the insanitary areas of the metropolis and employ a clerk and a peon to work under the health officer H.M. Crake.[59] By the Government of India Act, 1919, public health became a provincial subject and was placed under the control of the provincial government. In 1921, the Public Health Department was established as a part of a local self-government initiative. In the *Proceedings* of the Calcutta Municipality there was mention of employment of one clerk at Rs.50 and one peon at Rs.10 per month to inquire into the insanitary areas of the metropolis as a preliminary step.[60] In the *Annual Report* on the operations of the CIT for 1921–2, it was stated that two sites in Manicktala and Paikpara had been acquired where plots could be sold to people who were displaced by the works of the CIT.[61] In the case of re-housing, the issues of proper ventilation and sanitary condition of the dwellers were observed carefully. In a questionnaire session of a proceeding dating to January 1921, the spread of *kala-azar* in Calcutta was addressed. It also mentioned that the number of deaths due to *kala-azar*, as recorded in 1920, was 162 and that the average number of deaths from *kala-azar* during the preceding three years was 90. The cause behind this increase in deaths was the influx of people into the urban area for treatment.[62] A resolution dealing with the prevalence of *kala-azar* in Bengal was issued and grants of varying range from Rs.500 to Rs.700 were made to all district boards and the two municipalities of Howrah and Dacca for anti-*kala-azar* work during 1923–4. In the first All India Sanitary Conference (Bombay, 1911), Kailash Chandra Bose, LMS, in a paper titled 'Spread of Tuberculosis in Calcutta', showed the high prevalence of tuberculosis in the city. Anti-hookworm investigations were also made in 1921. While cholera was endemic at that time, government reports claimed it to be the most easily controlled disease as it was not contagious. It was stated that, to prevent the spread of cholera the supply of water had to be guarded against infection.[63] In contrast, the spread of leprosy was not as easily controlled. The Lepers Act, 1898, was extended to the municipal areas in Calcutta including Cossipore, Chitpore, Manicktala, the south suburbs, Tollygunge, Garden Reach, and Howrah. The Albert Victor Leper Asylum was built under this Act in 1901.[64] From 1916 to 1918, almost 718 pauper lepers in Calcutta were admitted to the asylums out of which 468 lepers were allowed to leave after the treatment. The section 431 to 447 of the Calcutta Municipal Act, 1923 entirely devoted to the prevention of infectious diseases among which leprosy was very significant. In fact, malaria, small-pox, tuberculosis, leprosy all were the evils with whom the colonial government had to fight. S.W. Goode had mentioned that though previously there was no statutory power of the Justices of Peace to apply municipal funds for the construction and maintenance of the hospitals, by 1913–1914 grants for the hospitals and dispensaries increased suddenly.[65]

The government was concerned about environmental pollution due to smoke and unclean water. Earlier, in 1896, the *British Medical Journal* noted that the drainage system of the town area was extremely defective.[66] Later, the Bengal Smoke Nuisance Act, which was framed in 1905 'for the abatement of nuisances rising from the smoke of furnaces or fire-places in the towns and suburbs of Kolkata and in Howrah and other areas of Bengal', was passed as the first law for the protection of nature in India.[67] At this time, Bengal was caught up in the widespread mass movement that followed the partition of the state. Amidst this turmoil, the Bengal Smoke Nuisance Act's main purpose was supposedly to preserve the dazzling whiteness of the white marble structure of Victoria Memorial.[68] The British were serious about the implementation of the Act. An independent 'Smoke Nuisance Commission' was set up under the Commissioner of the Presidency Range. Its functioning was supervised by the Chief Inspector of Smoke Nuisances. The commission was, however, later merged with the West Bengal Pollution Control Board after Independence. During this long process of legalization and progress, private companies had a sort of understanding with the government regarding commercial benefits. The license section of the Calcutta Corporation issued licenses to registered automobiles and asked them to pay taxes as a matter of surveillance.[69]

Electrification was one of the major areas where the efforts of the colonial government was instrumental. After the enactment of the Calcutta Electric Lightening Act in 1895, the most notable incident in the history of electrification in the city was the arrival of the Prince and Princess of Wales on the night of 3 January 1906 which witnessed major lighting works. In Bengal Act No. V of 1911 the executive board of the CIT was instructed to provide lighting facilities in all streets at night. From 1895 (with the enactment of the Calcutta electric Lighting Act) to 1910 street lighting was in the hands of private contractors. In 1910, the Calcutta Corporation began the important task of creating its own Lighting Department which assumed the management of lighting the entire city.[70] As the twentieth century was a very stimulating period due to the number of national as well international political upheavals, the indigenous population was very attentive towards the workings of the colonial government. A plethora of references are found in contemporary vernacular periodicals like *Bamabodhini* and *Bijoli* which indicated the indigenous people's concern for urban development. The *Bamabodhini* writes in August 1905 that a budget of 8 or 9 crores had been estimated for the purpose of the development of the city, of which the government would pay only Rs.50,000. The paper commented critically that the remainder of the expense would be collected from jute exports, income tax, imposition of taxes on fuel wood, and increase of railway fares and house taxes.[71] In an article title 'Kolkatar Unnatisadhon' or 'Development of Calcutta' in the *Bamabodhini*, dated April 1906, it was stated that Lord Curzon had hindered the urban development of Calcutta by partitioning Bengal.[72] In spite of such public opinion, the developmental and commercial initiatives of the government continued throughout the twentieth century. In the *Bijoli*, dated 22 April 1921, advertisements were published by the government for the sale of excess lands between Russa Road and Kalighat Road. In the same paper, regular advertisements were given by the Calcutta Corporation, asking for the rents of well-ventilated and electrified shops.[73]

The notion of 'improvement' as applied in the context of the colonial structure always leaves space for criticism. 'Improvement' and 'development' were often seen as intrusions by the colonial government in the everyday lives of the indigenous people. The idea of establishing trsuts in the colonies was also criticized in Britain, as reflected in the poems of William Blake and William Wordsworth. On the other hand, the various projects and schemes undertaken by the Calcutta Corporation and the CIT regarding re-housing, transport, electrification, and sanitation were very effective in making Calcutta one of the world's most prominent city at the time. Adaptation and acculturation were the processes through which the colonial government and the indigenous people interacted in twentieth-century Calcutta. The story of urbanization was not only an episode of continuous growth or of perpetuating decay. It was neither a story of the binary relationship between the colonizer and the colonized. There were multi-layered elements of development and crisis that affected all social layers according to their connections with the city. Beneath these elements lay the macro-history of the gradual collapse of the human environment, endangering our existence on the planet. The present chapter is a discussion on the land, houses, diseases, electricity, and the automobiles that had a 'presence' in the general landscape of Calcutta, and I have included all these issues in terms of 'statism', 'overcrowding', 'misutilization', 'excesses of science', 'infection', and 'environmental pollution'. The analysis exposes the contradictions of a colonial government to deal with fulfilling its own financial or imperial imperatives as well as the requirements for development and hygiene in a growing city.

Notes

1. Matthew Gandy, 'From Urban Ecology to Ecological Urbanism: An Ambiguous Trajectories', *Royal Geographical Society*, vol. 47, no. 2, 2015, pp. 150–61.

2. Benoy Ghose, 'Colonial Beginnings of Calcutta: Urbanisation without Industrialisaton', *The Economic Weekly*, 1960, pp. 1256–9.

3. Rajat Kanta Ray, 'Civil Society and Politics: Bengal (1905–1927)', in *A Comprehensive History of Modern Bengal: (1700–1950)*, vol. III, ed. Sabyasachi Bhattacharya, Delhi: Primus Books, 2020, pp. 232–6.

4. S.N. Sen, 'The Pioneering Role of Calcutta in Scientific and Technical Education in India', *Indian Journal of History of Science*, vol. 29, no. 1, 1994, pp. 41–7.

5. Mark Harrison and Biswamoy Pati, 'Social History of Health and Medicine: Colonial India', in *The Social History of Health and Medicine in Colonial India*, ed. Biswamoy Pati and Mark Harrison, New York: Routledge, 2009, pp. 5–6.

6. Aishwaryarupa Majumdar, 'Medical Education on the Colonial Periphery: A Study of the Medical Institutions in Patna and Dacca', vol. 53, no. 1, 2018, p. 35.

7. 'The Calcutta University and Science', *Calcutta Review*, 1864, pp. 1–5.

8. *Hundred Years of the University of Calcutta*, Chapter III, Calcutta, University of Calcutta Press, 1957, pp. 71–128.

9. *Chikitsa Sammilani*, vol. 8, 1891, p. 12.

10. Pradip Sinha, *Calcutta in Urban History*, Calcutta: Firma KLM, 1978.

11. *Swasthya Samachar*, 1319 (BS 300).

12. Mark Harrison, *Climate and Constitutions: Health, Race, Environment and British Imperialism in India, 1600–1850*, New Delhi: Oxford University Press, 1999, p. 154.

13. Roy Porter, *Disease, Medicine and Society in England, 1550–1860*, London: Macmillan, 2009, pp. 48–60.

14. Ibid. For details see Edwin Chadwick and O.A. Checkland, eds., *The Poor Law Report of 1834*, London: Penguin, 1974.

15. Partho Datta, 'Ranald Martin's Medical Topography (1837): Emergence of the Public Health in Calcutta', in *The Social History of Health and Medicine in Colonial India*, ed. Biswamoy Pati and Mark Harrison, New York: Routledge, 2009, pp. 15–28.

16. S.W. Goode, *Municipal Calcutta: Its Institutions in their Growth and Origin*, Edinburgh: The Corporation of Calcutta, T & A Constable, 1916, p. 226.

17. Ibid., p. 228.

18. *Annual Report of the Sanitary Commissioner with the Government of India, 1895*, Calcutta: Office of the Superintendent of Government Printing, India, 1896, pp. 144–5.
19. *Proceedings of the Municipal Department (Sanitation)*, Proceeding no. 3–4, File no. SE/1, Calcutta, 7 January 1911.
20. Mahua Sarkar and Subhasis Biswas, eds., *Glimpses of Environmental History*, Kolkata: Alphabet Books, 2018, pp. 9–20.
21. Debjani Bhattacharyya, *Empire and Ecology in the Bengal Delta: The Making of Calcutta*, United Kingdom: Cambridge University Press, 2018, p. 5.
22. Rila Mukherjee, 'The Making of Maritime Economy: Bengal, 1600–1800', in *A Comprehensive History of Modern Bengal: (1700–1950)*, vol. I, ed. Sabyasachi Bhattacharya, Kolkata: Primus Books, 2020, pp. 164–7.
23. Kabita Ray, *History of Public Health: Colonial Bengal (1921–1947)*, Calcutta: K. P. Bagchi and Co., 1998.
24. Monidip Chatterjee, 'Town Planning in Calcutta: Past, Present and Future', in *Calcutta the Living City*, vol II: The Present and Future, ed. Sukanta Chaudhuri, New Delhi: Oxford University Press, 1990, pp. 131–7.
25. Calcutta High Court, In Re: Manick Chand Mahata vs the Corporation of Calcutta And.... on 16th February, 1921, see https://indiankanoon.org/doc/1640415, accessed 19 November 2021.
26. Chris Furedy, 'British Tradesmen of Calcutta (1830–1900): A Preliminary Study of their Political and Economic Roles', in *Women Politics and Literature in Bengal*, ed. C.B. Sealy, East Lansing: Asian Studies Center, Michigan State University, 1981, pp. 43–62.
27. Tirthankar Roy, *India in the World Economy from Antiquity to the Present*, UK: Cambridge University Press, 2012, p. 9.
28. Rabindranath Tagore, *Rachanabali*, 9th khanda,

Santiniketan: Visvabharati, BS 1396/1985, pp. 414–15.

29. 'The Central Avenue: Calcutta's New Thoroughfare', in *Bengal Past and Present*, ed. Hiren Chakrabarti, Calcutta: Calcutta Historical Society, 1990, pp. 48–50.

30. Narayani Gupta, 'Urban Form and Meaning in South Asia: Perspectives from the Modern Era', *Studies in the History of Art*, vol. 31, 1993, pp. 243–52.

31. Marshall Berman, *All That is Solid Melts into Air: The Experience of Modernity*, New York: Penguin, 1988, pp. 164–6.

32. Dipesh Chakrabarty, 'Of Garbage, Modernity and the Citizen's Gaze', *Economic and Political Weekly*, 1992, pp. 541–7.

33. Quoted in Goode, *Municipal Calcutta*, p. 237.

34. Ibid., p. 148.

35. Ibid.

36. H. Beverley, *Report on the Census of Calcutta*, Cacutta: Bengal Secretariat Press, 1876, p. 51.

37. *The Municipal Administrative Reports for the Year 1875–1876 and 1900–1901.*

38. Sumit Sarkar, *Modern Times (India, 1880s–1950s): Environment, Economy, Culture*, New Delhi: Permanent Black, 2014, pp. 55–6.

39. Sally Sheard and Hellen Power, *Body and City: Histories of Urban Public Health*, United Kingdom: Ashgate, 2000, pp. 132–180.

40. C.H. Bompas, 'The Work of the Calcutta Improvement Trust', *Journal of the Royal Society of Arts*, vol. 75, no. 3868, 1927, p. 200.

41. Partho Datta, 'Calcutta on the Threshold of the 1940s', in *The Stormy Decades: Calcutta*, ed. Tanika Sarkar and Sekhar Bandyopadhyay, New Delhi: Social Science Press, 2015, p. 22.

42. Bompas, 'The Work of the Calcutta Improvement Trust', p. 201.

43. Henri Lefebvre, *The Production of Space*, Oxford: Blackwell, 1991, p. 337.
44. *Annual Report on the Operations of the Calcutta Improvement Trust for the year 1921–1922*, File no. M/3, 1922, p. 10.
45. Ibid., p. 11.
46. Ibid., p. 18.
47. Ibid.
48. Bompas, 'The Work of the Calcutta Improvement Trust', p. 209.
49. Ibid., p. 210.
50. H.V. Lanchester, 'Calcutta Improvement Trust: Precis of Mr. E.P. Richards' Report on the City of Calcutta', *The Town Planning Review*, vol. 5, no. 3, October 1914, p. 219.
51. Manimanjari Mitra, *Calcutta in the 20th Century: An Urban Disaster*, Calcutta: Asiatic Book Agency, 1990, pp. 44–5.
52. Bompas, 'The Work of the Calcutta Improvement Trust', pp. 210–11.
53. Sumanta Banerjee, *Memoirs of Roads: Calcutta from Colonial Urbanization to Global Modernizaton*, New Delhi: Oxford University Pres, 2016.
54. Lanchester, 'Calcutta Improvement Trust', pp. 120–1.
55. Ibid.
56. For details see Bishwendu Ghosh, 'From Palki to Automobile: Transport Revolution in Colonial Bengal', unpublished MPhil thesis, Jadavpur University, 2017.
57. Bijan Lal Mukherjee and Jatindra Nath Ghose, *Calcutta Improvement Act*, Calcutta: R. Cambray and Co., 1913, p. 45.
58. *Annual Report on the Operations of the Calcutta Improvement Trust for the Year 1921–1922*, pp. 10–15.
59. *Proceedings of the Hon'ble the Lieutenant-Government of Bengal, February, 1911 (Municipal*

Branch), File no. M 1C/2, Proceedings no. B 104-107, Calcutta, 1911, p. 6.

60. Ibid.

61. *Annual Report on the Operations of the Calcutta Improvement Trust for the Year 1921–1922*, Principal Officers of the Board on 31 March 1922.

62. *Proceedings of the Government of Bengal (Local Self-Government)*, January 1921, File – P.H. 2S–1, Proceeding no. 4–11, Calcutta, 1921.

63. *Proceedings of the Government of Bengal (Local Self-Government)*, January 1921, File no. P.H.Q. -20(1).

64. The Calcutta Municipal Act 1923, Bengal Act III of 1923, Legislative Department, Government of Bengal, Sections 431 and 436.

65. From the news page of West Bengal Pollution Control Board, Kolkata, 1985.

66. *The British Medical Journal*, vol. 2, no. 1867, 1896, pp. 1043–4.

67. Ibid.

68. *Bijoli*, vol. 16, no. 24, Baishakh 1328 BS 1921, page brittle.

69. The Calcutta Municipal Act 1923, Section 431 and 436.

70. Goode, *Municipal Calcutta*, p. 231. Also see Suvobrata Sarkar, 'The Electrification of Colonial Calcutta: Role of the Innovators, Bureaucrats and Foreign Business Organizations, 1880–1940', *Studies in History*, vol. 34, no. 1, pp. 48–76.

71. *Bamabodhini Patrika*, no. 504, 8th Kalpa, part II, Shrabon/August 1905 (BS 1312), p. 97.

72. *Bamabodhini Patrika*, no. 512, Chaitra/April 1906 (BS 1312), p. 112.

73. *Bijoli*, no. 23, Baishakh/April 1921 (BS 1328), page brittle.

2

Response of the Bhadralok

The development of urbanity alongside ecological degradation had a huge impact on the Bengali intelligentsia. The history of urbanization shows that beneath the multi-tiered elements of development lay the macro-history of the gradual collapse of the environment, endangering human existence. The reception of Western notions of science, sanitation, and public health in late nineteenth and early twentieth century Calcutta was never a linear process. The interpretation of the multi-tiered macro history reveals the true nature of this interaction between the colonial masters and the newly Western-educated intelligentsia. Here, the term intelligentsia encompasses both the bhadralok and bhadramahila. The colonial invocation of modern scientific education and notions of sanitation and public health had an immense repercussion in indigenous society. Moral legitimation for sanitation and public health had to be gained in a variegated cultural context. The main point here is about how the recipient culture absorbed Western notions in their social transformations. In many ways, the history of knowledge is always entwined with the history of contestation between the state and its people. This issue is also related to the broader history of the environment.

During the period 1817–1911, when institutional or official science was at its height, the contributions of the indigenous bhadralok were crucial to its development. Rammohun Roy was one of the earliest science enthusiasts of Bengal. The Derozians welcomed the entry of the western science. Another famous Brahmo intellectual, Akshay Kumar Dutta, once argued that a man has only two duties: one was to develop his physical body, and the second was to develop his knowledge.[1] These bhadralok were concerned with gaining the rational scientific knowledge of the West, which would help the former develop their society both physically and mentally.[2] I would argue that the nineteenth-century scenario saw a group of people, belonging mostly to the bhadralok, supporting and favouring Western styles of health and habitation in the city. There were series of government-mandated rules, regulations, and procedures that indirectly helped the intrusion of metropolitan medical science into the periphery. In the middle of the nineteenth century, the foundation and development of Calcutta University ushered in an era of growth of scientific knowledge systems.[3] The Bengali bhadralok had attained a kind of scientific cognition in the nineteenth century. Dhruv Raina and S. Irfan Habib have argued that the Bengali intelligentsia in the early nineteenth and late twentieth centuries marked a balanced progress between religion and science.[4] This argument had a definite relevance in nineteenth-century Bengal. Comtean positivism, which provided a basis for religion, had a huge impact on scientific as well as religious development during this time. Religious syncretism was backed by scientific progression. Rammohun Roy, Bankim Chandra Chattopadhyay, and Swami Vivekananda were representatives of this trend. They did not ignore the Upanishadic past and, at the same time, argued in favour of modern scientific progress. Subrata Dasgupta sees this as a shared cognitive identity with a 'schemata' of their own.[5] In *Bangadarshan*, edited by Bankim Chandra, there was mention of the Bharatbarshiya Bigyan Sabha, which advocated for the study of science as the necessity of the hour. There was also a search for the logical explanation of the universe and various celestial incidents. Science had been the main tool for European conquest and their mastery over science gave the colonial rulers the ability to dominate Indians.[6] There was a sense of introspection that enabled intellectuals like Bankim Chandra and Mahendralal Sircar to initiate search for scientific enquiry. They could comprehend the subjugated state of Indian society and culture under colonialism due to the lack of proper scientific sense. This realization led Ishwar Chandra Vidyasagar to propagate in favour of the invocation of Western education.

The modern, Western Baconian science ultimately involved development as well as destruction. This form of scientific knowledge failed to create a sustainable environment for all. Homi K. Bhabha has pointed out that cultural mimicry is an aspect of colonialism where the colonized tried to fit into the structure presented by the colonial rulers; thus, a 'grey zone' of contact emerged. Mary Louise Pratt has also described this as the 'contact zone', though she did not give any specific area for the study of said zone.[7] By applying this process of acculturation in the context of nineteenth and early twentieth-century Bengal, it can be argued that Calcutta, which was built on a long process of interaction with the colonial government, had also created a theocratical approach of universalism. This universalist approach of Rammohun Roy and Vidyasagar and their propagation in favour of Western education was also a specific product of the city. Calcutta was the place where nineteenth-century intellectuals found a way to cope with the scientific pace of the colonizers. In this narrative, it is evident that there were significant moments of change. There were initiatives of 'constructive imperialism', apparent through the founding of hospitals and other welfare works by the colonial government. Cases of 'imperial institutionalization', like the establishment of the Calcutta School of Tropical Medicine in 1914, had an 'independent' positive contribution towards the development of the public mindset. In the *Calcutta University Magazine*, dated January– December 1897, Rambrahma Sanyal was repeatedly mentioned as a reputed naturalist whose scientific merit espoused growing interest in science among indigenous intellectuals.[8] One of the most eminent personalities in this field was Mahendralal Sircar, who established the Indian Association for the Cultivation of Science (IACS) in 1876, with an ardent intention to advance scientific education. The *Bangadarshan* often published proposals to accumulate finances for Mahendralal Sircar.[9] The dire financial situation faced by him in establishing such organization can be aptly comprehended from a booklet titled *Indian Association for the Cultivation of Science: Its Short History and Urgent Needs* by Trailakya Nath Mukherji and Amrita Lal Sircar (1903).[10] It also faced opposition from a parallel movement launched by the Indian League for the foundation of an institute for technical education. The IACS propagated the need for self-sufficiency in technology in the face of colonial rule instead of mere theocratical education. All these instances proved that in spite of differences there was a consensus regarding the urgency of scientific education. In the Indian scenario, the Baconian rejection of institutionalized religion was not always applied to the newly developing scientific mind. Various articles in the *Dawn Society Magazine* were devoted to science, religion, and technology, which reflected the growing trend of nurturing science among the Bengali intelligentsia.[11] From Rammohun Roy and Syed Ahmad Khan to Mahendralal Sircar, the urge for refashioning age-old Indian culture through the adoption of Western science was at its height.

By the mid-nineteenth century, the city was drawn into the hub of colonial and trans-national capital investment, which brought more migrants to the city. The port facilities allowed the British to import finished goods and export raw materials and to expand international trading activities. Calcutta has been vividly cited in contemporary literary documents. Throughout the nineteenth century, the intelligentsia of Bengal portrayed the 'dirty' city in various ways, the language of expressions being satirical, varied, and interesting. They referred to pollution, dirt and the unhygienic situation in Calcutta in several tracts.

For example, Haridhan Dutta, the Commissioner of Ward no. 9, vigorously complained about the extremely unhygienic conditions of Calcutta hotels. He mentioned that the hoteliers had no morals and were only after money.[12] Durgadas Gupta writes about the unhygienic conditions of Calcutta schools in *Swasthya*.[13] He stated that the Sanitary Commission should take care of the ventilation and sanitation of schools. On 11 November 1899, an anonymous writer wrote an article in the third volume of *Swasthya* on titled 'Kolikata O Pallibash'. He stated that the 'Calcutta-mania' led to an increase of diseases and congestion of city which did not expand geographically.[14] He stated further that every day an average of more than 200 people were dying due to disease and pollution. Another anonymous writer argued in *Swasthya*[15] that dirty housing and unclean roads were responsible for the spread of the plague in Calcutta. Durgadas Gupta, the editor of *Swasthya*, mentioned that a death list showed that the number of deaths had increased in the previous five years due to the poor quality of underground water in the city. The literature also exposes the ambivalence and confusion of the local elite regarding the concept and nature of pollution, health, and urbanity. As far as the notion of public health was concerned, the British policy was one of modern improvement, but the Bengali people were divided regarding their allegiance to Western notions of public health and modern techniques of sanitation. The elite of Calcutta were confused about the concept of nature and the growing urban development launched by the Lottery Committee and subsequently by the Calcutta Improvement Trust (CIT). Strikingly, they were silent about the dirty part of the city and sometimes referred to it in satirical ways. The Bengali bhadralok, who were becoming health conscious, were not writing about the unhealthy nature of the slums or analysing the reasons behind the existence of these clumsy residential tragedies. They were adapting themselves to the new ethics of environmental sanitation and, at the same time, were clinging to their indigenous notions of sanitation and cleanliness. The bhadralok yearned for the past, wished for an improvement in the present, and lacked any plans for the future. Without reference to Bengali primary texts, one fails to understand these inner complexities of the colonized bourgeoisie. In the Bengali periodical *Swasthya*, a member of the bhadralok lamented that a sweetmeat-maker could not eat his own sweets and that a brahmin cook could not serve food in his own family.[17] He made these comments in connection with the poor habitable conditions of Calcutta. He mentioned resentfully that once upon a time, a place like 'Chowringhee' belonged to the people; but now they did not live there. They resided in those places 'where you have to keep your nostrils shut if you go there'.[18] His comments on Chowringhee exposed his perception of open spaces in the city: 'Chowringhee is the heaven of Calcutta; the place has no disease. Everyone should live there as the place is clean but few persons are living there, leaving their greed aside.'[19] The following comments were his suggestions for improvements:

Why not you make your place a Chowringhee of your own? Wherever you live make your own residence wide and beautiful; leave open spaces on the four sides of your residence, let your neighbours follow you. Then all the places in Calcutta will be a 'Chowringhee'; it is absolutely necessary to live in wide and open buildings in Calcutta, that is the only way to remain healthy in Calcutta.[20]

He provided definite suggestions for improving residential patterns:

If you cannot transform your villages to a Chowringhee then let all the wealthy people of the city make a healthy village like it in the open places which are lying outside near the city and there all will live happily. It is better to live there than staying in the garden houses (*baganbari*) for they will get all the facilities of a city by otherwise living in a healthy place. Moreover, this plan will beautify the city and extend the pride of the wealthy.[21]

An eminent intellectual, Peary Chand Mitra, in his book *Alaler Ghorer Dulal*, argued that only the English had the quality to make their houses neat and clean; due to their cleanliness diseases were gradually reduced in Calcutta. Along with this he also complained about his own people's callousness regarding hygiene. He referred to the stinking drains near the house of Babu Lakshmipati.[22] These responses show that there was a gradual adaptation and acculturation of the Bengali bhadralok to the Western notion of cleanliness. At the same time, there was a sense of abhorrence towards pollution, strikingly without any reference to the issue of poverty. Sivanath Sastri, in his renowned book *Ramtanu Lahiri O Tatkalin Bangasamaj*, argued that each locality Calcutta had one or two ponds and the dirty water in these water bodies bred insects that caused fever. People who were coming from the mofussils suffered from dysentery after living in Calcutta.

In the same period the city became the venue for the large foundational sites established for the building of offices and residences. In the contemporary texts these are referred as *lona-laga*, which refers to a disease that affected people with high intake of salt.[23] He writes that the situation had improved at the time of writing the book, i.e. 1903, and that there was no fever in the city. Mahendranath Dutta in his book *Kolikatar Purono Kahini O Protha*, argued that the city of Calcutta was infested with vultures and jackals during the nineteenth century. He also mentioned the disturbances of monkeys and the pathetic conditions of the mud-filled streets.[24] These scenes did not suit the mindset of the Bengali bhadralok, who were gradually becoming conscious about the benefits of the Western notion of hygiene. Surprisingly, this agenda was never taken up as an issue of active reform based on direct movement and action. A series of books and articles on this topic were published in vernacular languages from the mid-nineteenth century onwards, including *Swasthya, Swasthya Samachar, Chikitshok O Samalochok, Chikitsa Darpan,* and *Chikitsa Sammiloni*. The *Bamabodhini Patrika*, dated May 1905, showed some kind of concern regarding the spread of plague and also declared that the Calcutta municipality has announced a reward of 2 paisa for each dead rat.[25] Journals like *Probasi, Bangalakshmi, Bamabodhini,* and *Bangamahila* regularly published articles on health. In fact, 'public health' comprised an important aspect of 'print culture' in contemporary Bengal and had a deep impact on bhadralok society.[26]

Still, the roots of tradition and superstition were so deeply entrenched in the mindsets of people that it was very difficult to completely uproot old ideas from the daily lives of the masses. Bhubanchandra Basak, in his *Jalpanbidhi* (1884), suggested that people should follow the modern practice of drinking pure, unpolluted water. Other suggestions from the bhadralok ironically contained a combination of ayurvedic and allopathic practices, which hindered the development of pure Western habits. Similar combinations are found in articles like 'Rogir Proti Upodesh' (1907), by Satish Chandra Lahiri' and 'Abyartho Cholera O tadanusangik Upasarger Pratikar' (1928) by Arunoday Mukhopadhyay. Pradip Kumar Bose, in his compilation of late nineteenth-century Bengali periodicals, refers to the satirical pieces written about using a handkerchief instead of water after going to the toilet. He refers to numerous such writings on personal hygiene, cleanliness, food, water, use of disinfectants, and vaccination schedules for the improvement of public health and institutions. Still, there is a lacuna of indigenous writing on 'toilet habits' and the nature of toilets.[27] The Europeans were critical of this topic while the bhadralok were silent. This was significant from the perspective of environmental sanitation, and one can compile a 'history of odours' from the context of the varied sensorial perceptions of the people of Calcutta regarding toilet habits and sanitation. The bhadralok could not change their habits, while the government did not plan on creating open spaces for middle-income groups living in CIT buildings, though parks were built in subsequent periods. When the need for open spaces was perceived; it was too late.

The ecology of the city was dwindling. Moreover, scholars refer to the protests and resistance of the people against vaccinations and anti-plague measures. The clinging of people to the religious ritualism of goddess Sitala in the context of pox and Olabibi in the context of cholera, the regular use of amulets and the use of *totkas* or magical healing measures like *jalpoda, telpoda, jharphunk*, etc., indicated the power of superstitions and the strength of indigenous belief systems.[28] All these superstitions were retained by the bhadralok, leading to confusion regarding personal hygiene and public health. These themes were highlighted in the famous periodical *Swasthya*, published by Durgadas Gupta since 1901, exposing the ambivalence of the Bengali intelligentsia regarding maintenance of public hygiene. Greater emphasis was obviously given to new, Western ideas of cleanliness, but the nostalgia for 'indigenous' notions of purity was never completely lost. Later, the issues of civic amenities and public health became sites of political debates between the colonial government and the local elite, exposing the conflicts of opinions and interests among the intellectuals. It was also clear that no serious efforts were undertaken to improve the living condition of the common people. The entire colonial idea of environmental sanitation was based on the idea that local people were inherently unhealthy and knew nothing about the public health. This kind of idea certainly emerged with the growth of the city as a 'clean entity'. Public health programme of the nineteenth century retained its legacy in the twentieth century. Thus, colonial city of Calcutta offered a site of inner conflict between elites and the colonial rulers.

The indigenous elites exhibited a skepticism towards the interpretation of the western sanitary policy. That was an obvious consequence of colonial rule in Bengal. That was the consequence of the unplanned transformation of a trading mart into a giant city like Calcutta. Subhas Chandra Bose, the Mayor of Calcutta in the 1920s went in so far as comparing the polluted city with the politics of the polluted nation. The issues of civic amenities and public health gradually became sites of political debates between the colonial government and the local elite and the conflicts of opinions and interests within the intellectuals were exposed.

Sumanta Banerjee rightly argues in this context that public spaces in nineteenth-century Calcutta became new areas of contention between the rulers and the ruled. This was a conflict between the customary laws of the natives—the right to common space—and the new laws necessary for urbanization.[29] The British administrators imposed a code of conduct that criminalized some street professions like begging, soliciting by prostitutes on the main roads, or occupation of pavements by vendors and street entertainers. The rural poor who served as menial artisans and industrial workers in the city were forced to change their traditional habits and conform to the behavioural norms of citizenship that were enforced by the colonial rulers. Banerjee compared the streets of Calcutta and the black town in general with the backyard of Victorian London and found similarities in the government's mode of controlling public behaviour through municipal reforms and policing in Calcutta.[30] The reforms affected some of the sanitation-related habits of the city's poor. Previously, due to the availability of huge open spaces surrounding the villages, the people used to use the fields as their toilets, where human excreta transformed into natural fertilizers. This space was, naturally, not available in the city and the insufficient alternatives provided for the people did not suit their habits and cultural values. Conflicts arose over the use of toilets or construction of enclosed privies, *chalaghars* or thatched huts, and keeping of horned cattle, as the management of cattle waste proved to be a nuisance to public hygiene.[31] Thus, the rural population of Calcutta was forced to accept unfamiliar and alien urban norms without being provided alternative means of disposing waste or of building homes. They were also penalized for violating these norms.[32] Moreover, financial stringency did not permit the government to provide these people with better public amenities like clean public privies and better housing facilities. The situation remained unchanged even in the later periods. This resulted in a general degradation of public health and the spread of diseases. The majority of the intelligentsia looked at these issues from a distance, untouched and unaffected by such problems. They served as agents of beautification and urbanization, silently advancing the dominance of Western cultural superiority in their own mindsets. In spite of their own losses, the slum dwellers were made to understand that the beautification of the city would require their removal; the bhadralok often themselves appropriated the language of the other. Otherwise, in their general perception of purity, health, and pollution, they adhered to drastically different values that were related to their distinct religious and moral ethics.[33] The identity of the bhadralok were often merged with the slum dwellers regarding the perception of health habits, leading to the perception that neither was there an emergence of specific Western values in Calcutta at this time, nor was a concern for the overall maintenance of the city and the improvement of the general environment.

Notes

1. Mahua Sarkar, 'Pollution, Public Health and the People of Calcutta: The Nineteenth Century', *Journal of the Asiatic Society*, vol. LXII, no. 4, 2020, pp. 85–8.
2. Ibid. I have discussed this issue in the second chapter of this volume. For further details see, Mahua Sarkar, 'Environmental Sanitation and the *Bhadraloks* of Calcutta', in *Historical Essays in Memory of Professor Subhasis Biswas: Themes in Science, Technology, Environment and Medicine*, ed. Mahua Sarkar, Kolkata: Alphabet Books and Manohar, 2021, pp. 35–54.
3. Ibid.
4. Dhruv Raina and S. Irfan Habib, *Domesticating Modern Science: A Social History of Science and Culture in Modern India*, New Delhi: Tulika Books, 2004, pp. 120–81.
5. Subrata Dasgupta, *The Bengal Renaissance: Identity and Creativity from Rammohun Roy to Rabindranath Tagore*, New Delhi: Permanent Black, 2007, pp. 4–20.
6. Bankim Chandra Chattapadhyay, ed., *Bangadarshan*, Calcutta: Printed by Shri Brajamadhav Basu, 1873, pp. 232–40.
7. Homi K. Bhabha, *The Location of Culture*, London: Routledge, 1994; and Mary Louis Pratt, *Imperial Eyes:*

Travel Writing and the Transculturation, London: Routledge, 1992.

8. *Calcutta University Magazine: A Monthly Newspaper and Review*, vol. IV, January–December, 1897.
9. Chattopadhyay, *Bangadarshan*, p. 240.
10. Trailakya Nath Mukherji and Amrita Lal Sircar, *Indian Association for the Cultivation of Science: Its Short Histories and Urgent Needs*, Calcutta: Anglo-Sanskrit Press, 1903.
11. Raina and Habib, *Domesticating Modern Science*, pp. 120–40.
12. *Swasthya Samachar*, vol. 1, 1912 (BS 1319), p. 286.
13. *Swasthya*, vol. 3, no. 1, Baishakh/April–May 1899 (BS 1306), p. 194.
14. Ibid., pp. 325–6.
15. Ibid., pp. 27–9.
16. Ibid., p. 4.
17. *Swasthya*, vol. 3, no. 1, Baisakh/April-May 1900, (B.S. 1306), p. 6.
18. Ibid., translated by Professor Mahua Sarkar.
19. Ibid.
20. Ibid.
21. Ibid.
22. Peary Chand Mitra, *Alaler Gharer Dulal*, ed. Brajendranath Bandyopadhyay and Sajanikanto Das, Calcutta: Bangiyo Sahitya Parishad, 1993, p. 30.
23. Sivanath Sastri, *Ramtanu Lahiri o Tatkalin Brahmosamaj*, Calcutta: New Age Publishers, 1903, p. 47.
24. Mahendranath Dutta, *Kalikatar Puratan Kahini O Protha*, Calcutta: Mahendra Publishing Committee, 1884; repr., 1978, p. 20.
25. *Bamabodhini Patrika*, no. 501, year 43, part II, May 1905 (BS 1116), p. 29.
26. Pradip Kumar Bose, *Health and Society in Bengal: A Selection from the Late 19th Century Bengali Periodicals*, New Delhi: Thousand Oaks, 2006.

27. Ibid.
28. Arabinda Samanta, *Living with Epidemics in Colonial Bengal*, New York: Routledge, 2018, pp. 13–20.
29. Sumanta Banerjee, *The Wicked City*, New Delhi: Orient BlackSwan, 2009, pp. 229–36.
30. Ibid.
31. Ibid.
32. Ibid.
33. For the theory, see Mary Douglas, *Purity and Danger, An Analysis of Concepts of Pollution and Taboo*, USA: Routledge, 2003. For the Indian situation, see Debi Prasad Chattopadhyay, *Lokayata: A Study of Ancient Indian Materialism*, New Delhi: Peoples Publishing House, 2008. See also Debi Prasad Chattopadhyay, *Indian Philosophy: A Popular Introduction*, New Delhi: Peoples Publishing House, 1964.

3

Voices of the Bhadramahila

Western science and notions of public health in Bengali society advanced parallelly alongside the existing trend of social and educational reforms for women. The bhadralok launched protests against *kulinism*, polygamy and child marriage for women, and they wanted them to be educated them through various reform initiatives. As the nineteenth century proceeded, the two trends collided, resulting in the emergence of a patriarchal and protectionist idea regarding the development of the European concept of public health among women. The present chapter will analyse the nature of this collision of the two paradigms, through the prism of Bengali monthly journals like the *Bamabodhini Patrika* (hereafter *Bamabodhini*) and others.[1] Though much has been written on this topic, I feel there is a further necessity to collate the existing researches and deliver a micro-study of the scenario, based on primary documents. From its inception, the *Bamabodhini* declared a war against prevailing superstitions and adopted a scientific attitude towards life and living.[2] Its separate section of *bamarachana* (writings of women) launched early literary works of women in vernacular journalism.[3] The journal disseminated Western concepts of health and hygiene among women through its regular column on *swasthyaraksha* or maintenance of health. A major section of these thoughts contained discussions on cleanliness and sanitation, household medicine, motherhood, and childcare. In the pages of the *Bamabodhini*, the growth of Western education among women was reflected through the mention of European scientific notions of healthcare and preventive health measures. This had a gradual impact on the daily lives of women. The following comments were made in the introduction of the journal's first volume: 'Special attention will be given to those themes which will eradicate their faults and superstitions, so that the true and necessary knowledge will emerge and the best kind of mentality will guide all necessary issues' (translation mine).[4] In their daily lives, instead of following the traditional *panjika* or almanac time, the *Bamabodhini* instructed women to follow the clock-time of the west as that was scientific and hygienic. Thus, one writer Ramasundari Debi, in her article titled 'Somoy' or 'Time', regulated fixed times for work and leisure for women: 'In my opinion the housewives will be able to fulfill their duties if they follow the rules as instructed below: sleep for 7 hours, bathing and eating for 3 hours, domestic work, childcare and teaching for 7 hours, spiritual thinking, knowledge gathering and all other good works for 7 hours' (translation mine).[5] Special attention was given to 'discipline' and 'cleanliness' while running the household. These perceptions were emerging from the new Western notions of civic urbanity, distinctly different from the earlier models of village society. For instance, the reason behind cleaning one's clothes lay in the idea of eradicating germs. That is why the *Bamabodhini* provided advice about the body in the following way:

It is known from the science of the body that everyday an amount of half seer dirt comes out from the pores of our body. The pores lie fixed under the dirty clothes. Therefore the internal dirt cannot come out. Also, the body suffers from many diseases and the bad odour which comes out from the dirty clothes destroys the health of the mind and the body.[6] (translation mine)

For the maintenance of health, the *Bamabodhini* followed Western notions of cleanliness regarding *mukhaprakshalan* (washing of the face), *gatramarjana* (washing of the body), *snan* (bathing), *keshamarjana* (washing of the hair) and *suchi byabahar* (washing after toilet).[7] Kumudini Ray, in her article 'Hindu Narir Garhasthyadharma' (The Household Duties of a Hindu Female) stated that the compulsory household duty of a Hindu female consisted of cleaning, washing bed linens, dusting twice daily, and purifying drinking water.[8] Apart from this, hard work for the maintenance of general health was also emphasized. It was pointed out that one should not work excessively as that was injurious to health and that one should take rest after hard work.[9] Thus, the journal stressed a scientific method of work. According to the *Bamabodhini*, cooking was equivalent to a form of chemistry and all diets should be scientifically formulated for the improvement of health. Cooking or culinary sciences were mentioned as *pakvigyan* or *randhanik rasayan.* [10] A healthy diet for pregnant women was highlighted as it was argued that the good health of the parents would be infused within the unborn child. The best kind of room for a pregnant woman was prescribed thus:

All houses are not the same due to difference in standards; still the room which is the best from all standards should be preserved as the labour room for childbirth. That room should be wide with windows in the north and the south for the entry of pure air, and no place with bad odour should be kept near that room. The room where sunlight can enter will be the best place for delivery.[11] (translation mine)

An author in the *Bamabodhini* wrote a poem on the human digestive system. There, the mechanism of digestion was explained along with the formation of excreta.[12] In another article, the functioning of the vocal cords was described through a fusion of scientific knowledge and divinity. It was stated that healthy vocal cords were imperative to sign devotional songs.[13] The three important idioms of healthcare, as highlighted by the *Bamabodhini*, were 'cleanliness, motherhood and childcare'. In traditional Indian culture where motherhood was a woman's only ambition and where the most unfilial act was not giving birth to a son, childbirth was a focal point of every form of medical advice. In the articles of the journal, thus, there was great concern for the health of infants. In an article titled 'Matrishiksha hoite udhrito' or 'Lessons from Mothers', the writer mentioned various symptoms of certain illnesses that made children uncomfortable.[14] In 1913 (BS 1319), Charumati Devi wrote 'Infantile

Mortality and Mother's Responsibility', highlighting the unhealthy condition of the *sutikagriha* (the act of lying-in during childbirth) during delivery, which made the newborn prone to ailments. Even if they were saved by the grace of God, the dearth of proper shelter, pure air, and nutritious food hindered them from having a normal life. The middle- and upper-class families of Bengal hardly bothered about sanitation and personal cleanliness. They were unaware of the importance of pure water and air. According to Charumati Devi, all these factors led to frequent occurrence of diseases.[15] Moreover, she stated that women's education was the key to their emancipation. She appealed to the male members of society to take care of their female counterparts. The poor status of housewives and the prevalence of malnourished, badly clothed infants, perhaps evidenced the gender imbalance and discrimination inherent in contemporary Hindu society.[16] The importance of breastfeeding and use of filtered water were also highlighted to spread general awareness with regard to childcare.

A series of articles were regularly published in the *Bamabodhini* from July 1912 to August 1914 under the title 'Shishujibon o kinder garten' or 'Children's Life and Kindergarten'. These focused on the development of the brain function and senses of infants[17] and incorporated preschool educational approaches based on playing, singing, drawing, and social interaction as part of the transition from home to school. According to the writer, the primary duties of a mother after childbirth were to look after the child's health and education. It was suggested that both over-eating and under-eating were bad for the health of a child. The parents should always be conscious of a child's physical development.[18] The child should be bathed in lukewarm water; he/she should be dressed according to the weather. Children should also not be unnecessarily treated with medicine, for not healing naturally at this stage of development would cause harm to them later.[19] Emphasis was laid upon the maintenance of the 'good character' of the mother, the father, and the teacher as that would influence the character of the child.[20]

Apart from the *Bamabodhini*, another important journal of the nineteenth century, the *Bangamahila*, also espoused the notion of health awareness among women. This topic constituted an important part of the content of the journal. The necessity for good health among women along with the necessity for physicians to maintain their health has been described in various articles of this periodical. In the first volume of the *Bangamahila*, a routine and an examination syllabus for women was published by the principal of Chor-Bagan Balika Vidylaya. This syllabus mentioned a book called *Swasthya-Raksha*, written by Radhikaprasanna Mukhopadhyay.[21] In every volume of *Bangamahila* articles on health were compulsory, specifically regarding the maintenance of a mother's health and the correlation between the health of a child and its mother had been.[22]

An awareness of health and sanitation among women in the nineteenth century was crucial as they constituted an important part of the 'private sphere' of the Bengali intelligentsia. The above-mentioned discussions hastened the medicalization of childbirth, the sanitization of sex, and the management of children, thus confirming a new regime of intimacy of the self, to which women were also adapting.[23] Health and hygiene, thus defined within the parameters of motherhood and childcare, became feminist issues in later periods.[24] The *Bamabodhini* as well as the *Bangamahila*, however, had not completely discarded indigenous notions of health and medicine. There were ample references of herbal medicines in the name of g*riha-chikitsa* or home-treatment in the *Bamabodhini*. For example, stomach pain was supposed to be treated with a watery paste of curd, roots of Catechu and two burnt cloves that was then drunk through a cooking filter or *chaluni*.[25] Supriya Guha writes about Western ideas of healthcare:

The new ideas that became current among medical and paramedical personnel as well as among the 'informed public' were often received ideas (sometimes slightly dated) from Europe, but at other times, especially as we see them emerge in vernacular texts, they were refracted through culturally conditioned notions of the nature and role of woman (or, rather, 'woman') as well as issues of current political relevance.[26]

The two journals, thus, combined the Indian style of motherhood with Western ideas of science and healthcare.

The articles mentioned above exposed the complexities of womanhood in nineteenth and early twentieth-century Bengal. On the one hand, women, or more specifically the bhadramahila, were modelled by the patriarchy according to ideal, traditional notions of the household; on the other hand, women were being trained in modern ideas of science and healthcare in terms of hygiene and good health. In the application of medicine, these women drew from traditional as well as modern methods.[27] Maintenance of the household or family was the main reason behind the improvement of women's health. While this issue received importance, there was a sense of neglect towards individual physical desires. The Brahmo women were touched by the reformist impulse of their male counterparts but the majority of them were still dependent on men, both socially and economically. Politically as well, the 'home' became a symbol of *bharatiyatva* or Indianization and *jatiyatabad* or nationalism, and notions of health were framed accordingly. The emerging cultural identity of an Indian nationhood was infused into the new concern about Ayurveda, which became a metaphor for both Indianization and nationalism. Indigenous notions of health referring to Ayurveda as sources of treatment were detailed in contemporary medico journals. For example Binodbehari Dey, the editor of *Chikitshak*, stated that a person should follow the prescription of his own country; therefore, all the principles of Ayurveda were laid down in the journal.[28] The nationalist response was to construct a reformed tradition and defend it on the grounds of modernity. This created the image of a 'new woman' who was superior to Western women, traditional Indian women, and subaltern women. This new patriarchy invested women with the dubious honour of representing a distinctively modern national culture.[29] With the emergence of nationalist consciousness in Bengal, Indian womanhood, entrenched in the private sphere, glorified as subservient, docile and sacrificial, became an icon of nascent nationalist aspirations. The so-called scientific image of 'healthy', 'enlightened' women was largely influenced by Victorian bourgeois values of 'ideal couplehood'. At the same time, for a Brahmo man in the late nineteenth century, one's lifestyle was very significant. The womanly virtues that would help preserve the *grihadharma* or family piety, such as benevolence, love, patience, modesty, and chastity, were highlighted as essential feminine qualities, as distinct from those inherent in men. Sivanath Sastri, an eminent Brahmo leader, wrote that women should be imparted with education to maintain *grihadharma* and establish the household as a place where chaste characters could be built.[30] In 1893, during the thirtieth anniversary celebration of the *Bamabodhini*, Sastri, in his speech gave the examples of educated women behind social reforms and humanitarian works in England. He stated that these women were becoming a force to reckon within Parliament. He hoped that educated women in Bengal would in the future similarly fulfill their role in society.[31] Following these ideals, the *Bamabodhini* maintained the puritan, guardian-like approach towards woman's emancipation. Its conservative attitude was reflected in the issue of segregation of men and women. It published an article supporting the social segregation of the genders on the ground that close proximity of the sexes would bring impure thoughts and that segregation was in conformity with religious ethics.[32] Another Brahmo paper, the *Abalabandhab*, was more flexible in its approach and jeered at the *Bamabodhini*, saying that 'it would be even better if the men were to be kept in the old big island and the woman in

the new'.[33] This naturally incurred the displeasure of
the *Bamabodhini* which was reflected in its pages.[34]
Thus, there emerged a journalistic 'war' on the issue
of women's emancipation; however, in reality the
progress of women was not related to this war. In the
twentieth century, women (mainly from the upper and
middle classes) were gaining admission in schools,
colleges, jobs, and politics. Lower-class women were
working as labourers and prostitutes and had no voices
of their own. But they were not the target audience of
the *Bamabodhini* or the *Bangamahila*; their readers
mostly consisted of the *sadharon madhyabitta gharer
meye* or women of the common middle class.

Aside from issues of healthcare and sanitation
being reflected in such periodicals, it is difficult to
ascertain what women actually thought about their
health or how far they accommodated Western ideas
of hygiene and cleanliness in their lives. Brahmo
women may have had a separate voice, distinct from
their menfolk, regarding issues of women's health,
particularly women's physical condition in their in-
laws' residences or the rising numbers of childbirth.
However, these historical gaps have yet to be filled.
Still, the articles published in the *Bamabodhini* and
Bangamahila were no small step. A new discourse
was produced unifying the old and the new. Women
had to walk a long, complicated path throughout the
twentieth century to gain emancipation. A positive
aspect of this was that the health of women improved
significantly. Thus, the health initiatives undertaken
by the *Bamabodhini* and the *Bangamahila* were not
insignificant, if one takes a long view of women's
history in India. Greater emphasis was obviously

given to new Western ideas of cleanliness, but the nostalgia for 'indigenous' notions of purity was never completely lost. Later, issues of civic amenities and public health became sites of political debates between the colonial government and the local elite. It was also clear that no serious efforts were undertaken to improve the living condition of common, lower-class women.

The colonial idea of environmental sanitation was based on the concept that the native population was inherently unhealthy and knew nothing about public health. This idea certainly emerged with the growth of the city as a 'clean entity'. Public health programmes in the nineteenth century retained their legacy in the twentieth century. Thus, the colonial city of Calcutta offered a site of inner conflict between elites and colonial rulers on the topics of healthcare, sanitation, and hygiene.

Notes

1. The *Bamabodhini Patrika*, edited by Umesh Chandra Dutta and later by Sukumar Dutta was published in Kolkata from 1863 to 1922. For details, see Brajendranath Bandyopadhyay, *Deshiyo Samoyikpatrer Itihas*, vol. I, Calcutta: Ranjan Publishing House, Bangiya Sahitya Parishad, 1935; Benoy Ghose, *Samoyikpatre Banglar Samajchitra*, vol. V, revd. edn., Calcutta: Papyrus, 1983; Swapan Basu and Muntasir Mamun, eds., *Dui Sataker Bangla Sangbad Samoyikpatra*, Kolkata: Pustak Bipani, 2005.

2. Bharati Ray, *Nari o Paribar: Bamabodhini Patrika*, Calcutta: Pustak Bipani, 1999; Bharati Ray, *Sekaler*

Nari Siksha: Bamabodhini Patrika, Calcutta: Women's Studies Research Centre, Calcutta University,1994.

3. For details, see Tanusree Sengupta, 'Bamabodhini Patrika: Samajbhabna o Sahityaprasanga', unpublished PhD thesis, Santiniketan, Visva-Bharati, 2012.

4. Brajendranath Bandyopadhyay, *Bangla Samoyikpatra*, vol. I, 4th edn., Calcutta: Bangiya Sahitya Parishad, 1972, p. 188.

5. Ramasundari Ghosh, 'Samay', *Bamabodhini Patrika*, Kartick 1881 (BS 1288), page brittle. See also Parbati Basu, 'Adarsha Grihini', *Bamabodhini Patrika*, Falgun 1880 (BS 1287, pp. 348–9).

6. 'Swasthyaraksha', *Bamabodhini Patrika*, Poush 1863 (BS 1270), pp. 53–4.

7. 'Swasthyaraksha', *Bamabodhini Patrika*, Falgun 1863 (BS 1270), pp. 77–80.

8. Kumudini Ray, 'Hindu Narir Garhasthya Dharma', *Bamabodhini Patrika*, Poush 1894, (BS 1301), p. 359; Meredith Borthwick, *The Changing Role of Women in Bengal, 1849–1905*, Princeton: Princeton University Press, 1984, p. 207. Also cited in Sujata Mukherjee, *Gender, Medicine and Society in Colonial India*, New Delhi: Oxford University Press, 2017, p. 109.

9. 'Sharirik Swasthyabidhan', *Bamabodhini Patrika*, Jaisthya 1867 (BS 1274), p. 514.

10. 'Garhasthya Shiksha', *Bamabodhini Patrika*, Srabon 1881 (BS 1288), p. 116.

11. 'Dhatrividya', *Bamabodhini Patrika*, Agrahayan 1867 (BS 1274), p. 636.

12. *Bamabodhini Patrika*, Ashad 1871 (BS 1278), p. 50.

13. Ibid., pp. 89–94.

14. Ibid.

15. *Bamabodhini Patrika*, Agrahayan 1912 (BS 1319), pp. 244–5.

16. Ibid.

17. *Bamabodhini Patrika*, Jaisthya 1914 (BS 1321), p. 34.

18. 'Sishupalan', *Bamabodhini Patrika*, Magh 1869 (BS 1276), p. 190.
19. 'Sishuder Ahar', *Bamabodhini Patrika*, Baisakh 1866 (BS 1273), p. 246.
20. 'Sishusantaner prati Matar Kartabya', *Bamabodhini Patrika*, Kartick 1892 (BS 1299), p. 220.
21. *Bamgamahila*, vol. I, no. 1, Baishakh 1875 (BS 1282), pp. 66–7.
22. See *Bangamahila*, vols. I–II.
23. Aparajita Dhar, 'Women's Writing and Health in Colonial Bengal', *Murmurs of History: Essays in Honour of Professor Ranjit Sen*, ed. Prasanta Mandal and Anjona Chattopadhyay, Kolkata: Progressive Publishers, 2018, p. 302.
24. Antoinette Burton, *Dwelling in the Archive: Women Writing House Home and History in Late Colonial India*, New York: Oxford University Press, 2003, p. 8.
25. *Bamabodhini*, 1870, p. 51.
26. Supriya Guha, 'The Nature of Women: Medical Ideas in Colonial Bengal', *Indian Journal of Gender Studies*, vol. 3, no. 1, 1996, p. 23.
27. A series of articles were published on 'Panchan o Mustijog' (Indigenous Concoction and Exercise). See *Bamabodhini*, Baisakh 1895 (BS 1302), for instance.
28. *Chikitsak*, vol. 3, no. 4, 1889 (BS 1296), p. 64.
29. Partha Chatterjee, *The Nation and its Fragments*, New York: Oxford University Press, 1995.
30. Sivanath Sastri, *Grihadharma*, Calcutta: Sadharan Brahmo Samaj, 1889; repr., 1941, p. 17.
31. *Bamabodhini Patrika*, Aswin 1893 (BS 1300), p. 164.
32. 'Abalabandhab', *Bamabodhini Patrika*, Ashad 1871 (BS 1278), p. 96.
33. Ibid.
34. Ibid.

Conclusion

Colonialism is itself a cultural process. The interaction between Western and indigenous systems of health and sanitation gave birth to new structures of development in nineteenth and the early twentieth-century Bengal. The congenial relationship between industrialization and environment needs to be understood in retrospection in this regard. The transition from mercantile capitalism to industrial capitalism led to another parallel trend of consciousness regarding environmental degradation in the metropole in the early nineteenth century. This trend was transplanted in the colonial periphery with the injunction of indigenous norms. The relentless efforts to build a planned city and the minute observations on every aspect of public health and sanitation made by the colonial masters were reflections of this realization. In 1899, Lord Curzon brought in a new legislative measure, namely the Calcutta Corporation Act, by which the strength of the elected members of the Corporation was reduced and that of the official members increased. Curzon gave more representation to the English over the Indians in the organization. A strong feeling of resentment developed among the Indian members against Curzon's anti-people measures. These political affairs ultimately led to the rise of the Swarajya Party. But the growth of nationalist politics was not directly linked with environmental awareness. Though the knowledge about the environment existed in the precolonial period, its concrete institutionalization in colonial times made it more comprehensive. The mindset of the colonized gentry gradually changed. Later, in the late 1920s, the concepts of health and sanitation along with civic development formed some of the most debated issues among the rulers as well as the ruled. Each of these parties moulded their ideas according to their needs and adapted them to their immediate surroundings.

Urban development alters the flora, fauna and human population of the land and has long-lasting effects on nature. Though not apparently linked, the history of urban development and the history of environment are minutely interwoven. Both require the study of ecosystems that include humans living in cities and urbanizing landscapes. It is an emerging, interdisciplinary field that aims to understand how human and ecological processes can coexist in human-dominated systems. These processes can help societies with their efforts to become more sustainable. At present the notion of sustainable development has emerged in this context to provide a solution to the situation. It denotes a balance between development of urban areas and protection of the urban environment. Within the rubric of sustainable development, special attention is given to equity in employment, providing shelter to all, establishing basic social infrastructure for the improvement of public health, and providing basic civic amenities to all, irrespective of caste, community, and class. This demonstrates that there was a lack of sustainable development between 1817 and 1923. According to John Bellamy Foster, there are inherent contradictions between capitalism and sustainability.[1] With the growth of capitalism, there was a perceptible shift towards sustainability and the effort to maintain the latter was just a guise to secure the unhindered growth of competition.

Capitalism as a universalizing system nurtures the notion of free trade. If seen against the limited resources of our planet, it becomes evident that capitalism and environmental sustainability can never be on the same foot.[2] Narayani Gupta mentions that the nineteenth-century capitalist fetish with urbanization as a sign of progress was problematic and often indicated not good health but underdevelopment.[3] Amiya Kumar Bagchi has also written about the environmental destruction and loss of lives caused by armed capitalism.[4] In this volume, I have explored significant moments of change initiated by 'constructive imperialism', evident through the founding of hospitals and streets in Calcutta throughout the nineteenth century. Also significant were cases of 'imperial institutionalization' like the establishment of the Medical College in 1835 and the Calcutta School of Tropical Medicine in 1914, which had an 'independent' positive contribution towards the development of urban ecology. But ultimately, the internal tensions within the colonial administration exposed the differences regarding the implementation of a single-minded public policy and threatened the future of a 'clean environment'. The colony became a construct of experimentation and research that was hampered by differences in attitudes towards development. The story of the period between 1817 and 1923 is one of demolition, displacement, and de-settlement without a proper scheme. The reports of C.H. Bompas also addressed this problem, writing that the question of the hour pertained to which issue the Calcutta Improvement Trust should first concentrate on.[5] Ultimately, the grand narrative of the gradual 'Indianization' of Western urban health measures in the 'tropical' city of Calcutta could hardly improve the environmental scenario of the city. The economic and social hierarchy within the patterns of urbanization in colonial Calcutta remained a permanent blockade for balanced ecological development. It can be said that with the advent of colonial modernity there was a paradigm shift in the notion of development itself. This shift was not compatible with the indigenous systems, which in turn affected the environmental balance or the idea of preservation. One may argue that it was too early to think about environmental disaster, but from the beginning of the Industrial Revolution in Europe, social philosophers were expressing their anxieties about the consequent destruction of nature. The following atmospheric record of 1913 (Plate 2) shows that England had already become conscious of recording its atmospheric pollution in a scientific way, which was never applied in a colony like India.

The various measures taken by the colonial government indicate the fact that the administrators were well aware of this relationship between their developmental efforts and general environmental degradation. Ideas about sustaining the colony emerged much later. When Western and Indian philosophers like Mahatma Gandhi, Rabindranath Tagore, Patrick

382 THE LANCET,]   A MONTHLY RECORD OF ATMOSPHERIC POLLUTION.   [MARCH 9, 1918

A MONTHLY RECORD OF ATMOSPHERIC POLLUTION.

METEOROLOGICAL OFFICE: ADVISORY COMMITTEE ON ATMOSPHERIC POLLUTION: SUMMARY OF REPORTS FOR THE MONTHS ENDING

August 31st, 1917.

Place.	Rainfall in millimetres.	Insoluble matter.			Soluble matter.		Total solids.	Included in soluble matter.		
		Tar.	Carbonaceous other than tar	Ash.	Loss on ignition.	Ash.		Sulphate as (SO_3).	Chlorine (Cl).	Ammonia (NH_3).
ENGLAND.										
Leicester	117	0·27	4·50	8·41	1·95	4·63	19·76	2·33	0·60	0·26
London—										
Meteorological Office	181	0·10	1·42	3·10	4·34	7·24	16·20	3·07	0·89	0·27
Embankment Gardens	94	0·07	4·27	7·83	2·14	6·29	20·59	2·92	0·94	0·15
Finsbury Park	117	0·09	3·08	11·32	1·87	5·39	21·75	2·53	1·05	0·14
Ravenscourt Park	104	0·10	1·96	9·97	0·66	4·19	16·87	1·71	1·04	0 15
Southwark Park	62	0·01	2·14	7·08	2·11	5·52	16·86	2·84	0·75	0·11
Wandsworth Com.	39	0·01	0·21	0·60	0·51	2·40	3·73	1 07	0·43	0·05
Golden Lane	100	0·11	2·72	4·16	3·23	5·65	15·87	3·01	0·93	0·28
Malvern	142	Nil.	0·23	1·13	0·64	1·94	3·94	1·08	0·15	0·07
Manchester—										
Queen's Park	167	—	—	—	—	—	14·30	—	—	—
School of Technology	231	—	—	—	—	—	21·80	—	—	—
Newcastle-on-Tyne	182	0·13	4·19	10·35	5·81	7·99	23·50	3·80	0·77	0·49
Rochdale	—	—	—	—	—	—	34·63	—	—	—
St. Helens	141	0·41	5·78	16·77	3·03	6·14	32·13	3·39	1·55	0·28
SCOTLAND.										
Coatbridge	106	0·09	2·46	7·81	2·45	5·80	18·61	2·75	0·30	0·23
Glasgow—										
Alexandra Park	81	0·03	2·28	4·21	1·45	4·43	12·40	2·43	0·16	0·16
Bellahouston Park	91	0·03	2·05	2·67	1·37	3·92	10·04	1·82	0·14	0 05
Blythswood sq.	91	0·27	2·90	6·08	2·07	4·52	15 64	2·69	0·16	0·25
Botanic Gardens	96	0·07	2·27	3·90	1·83	3·90	11·97	2·31	0·17	0·09
Richmond Park	96	0·01	2·52	7·42	1·64	3·80	15·39	2·54	0·15	0 04
Ruchill Park	89	0·06	1·94	8·22	0·90	6·48	17·60	2·48	0·14	0·12
South Side Park	88	0·05	1·08	3·01	1·69	4·13	9·96	2·05	0·10	0 02
Tollcross Park*	107	0·21	5·86	128·43	1·97	4·47	140·94	2·56	0·10	0·02
Victoria Park*	89	0·19	1·28	4·03	0·98	2·52	9·00	1·70	0·12	0·23

Sept. 30th, 1917.

Place.	Rainfall in millimetres.	Insoluble matter.			Soluble matter.		Total solids.	Included in soluble matter.		
		Tar.	Carbonaceous other than tar	Ash.	Loss on ignition.	Ash.		Sulphate as (SO_3).	Chlorine (Cl).	Ammonia (NH_3).
ENGLAND.										
Leicester	46	0·08	2·32	4·94	1·87	1·69	10·82	1·05	0·29	0·12
London—										
Meteorological Office	29	0·05	1·41	1·12	0·38	3·22	6·18	0.83	0·22	0·08
Embankment Gardens†	62	0·82	19 46	189·70	5·31	16·21	231·50	5·30	1·34	0·08
Finsbury Park	47	0·09	3·07	2·86	1·64	2·83	10·45	1·58	0·35	0·05
Ravenscourt Park	62	0·01	2·06	7·77	1·49	2·77	14·10	1·00	0·32	0 14
Southwark Park	41	0·03	1·13	3·60	3·07	4·29	12·11	2 72	0·45	0·14
Wandsworth Com.	32	0·01	0·36	1·09	0·84	1·66	3·96	0·71	0·19	0·02
Golden Lane	51	0·02	2 01	2·93	1·84	2·66	9·46	1·58	0 36	0 14
Malvern	46	tr.	0·08	0·08	0·43	0 74	1·34	0·38	0·07	0 01
Manchester—										
Queen's Park	29	—	—	—	—	—	11·50	—	—	—
School of Technology	44	—	—	—	—	—	18·20	—	—	—
Newcastle-on-Tyne	35	0·08	4·72	12·51	1·40	3·22	21·93	1·42	0·21	0 07
Rochdale	—	—	—	—	—	—	34·63	—	—	—
St. Helens	41	0·17	2·43	4·74	1·65	4·95	13·94	2·39	0·78	0 12
SCOTLAND.										
Coatbridge	60	0·07	1·63	5·87	2·32	4·40	14·29	2·60	0·34	0 15
Glasgow—										
Alexandra Park	38	0·37	1·48	4·61	0·83	3·31	10·60	1 46	0·15	0 04
Bellahouston Park	40	0·11	1·15	2·09	1·04	3·16	7·55	1·02	0·23	0 01
Blythswood sq.	47	0·43	1·86	4·61	0·94	3·50	11·34	1·82	0·07	0 14
Botanic Gardens	49	0·07	1·89	3·26	1·22	4·14	10·58	1·77	0·26	0 01
Richmond Park	44	0·01	1·32	6·30	2·51	2·29	12·43	1·92	0·12	0 10
Ruchill Park	54	0·18	1·39	3·92	1·70	2·57	9·76	2·20	0·13	0 09
South Side Park	59	0·12	1·11	2·38	1·47	5·18	10·26	1·31	0·10	0 03
Tollcross Park	42	0·10	0·83	3·41	1·08	2·32	7·74	1 62	0·09	0 02
Victoria Park	50	0·40	1·70	2 32	2·95	1 40	8 77	1·32	0·11	0 14

* The large amount of ash is attributed to sand thrown into the gauge by boys.   † The large amount of ash is attributed to abnormal dust.   tr. = trace.

"Tar" includes all matter insoluble in water but soluble in CS₂. "Carbonaceous" includes all combustible matter insoluble in water and in CS₂. "Insoluble ash" includes all earthy matter, fuel, ash, &c. One metric ton per sq. kilometre is equivalent to: (a) Approx. 9 lb. per acre; (b) 2·56 English tons per sq. mile; (c) 1 g. per sq. metre; (d) 1/1000 mm. of rainfall.

The personnel of public health authorities concerned in the supervision of these examinations and of the analytical work involved remains the same as published in previous tables.

Plate 2: Monthly record of environmental pollution, 1913

Source: *The Lancet, A Monthly Record of Atmospheric Pollution*, 1918, p. 382, see https://doi.org/10.1016/S0140-6736(00)53690-3, accessed 19 September 2021.

Geddess, and Leonard Elmherst expressed their alternative thoughts about urbanization and the environment, it was already too late.

Calcutta as a city had always been an enigma in the history of the environment. Though it was once the capital of the British Empire and the administrative headquarters of the colony, it functioned as a nexus between the colonial power and the innumerable, poverty-stricken, exploited masses. Despite the fact that its existence became a focus of discourse through imperial design, its growth was blatantly marked by commercial utility and lacuna of real planning. As a result, its urban identity was never shaped properly. No ecofriendly society emerged in the city, while serious intellectual discussions about how to make the city 'clean' and 'green' continued in vain. Calcutta represented a rural-urban continuum, a 'dirty' paradise with vast areas of underdevelopment. The municipal archives show how all efforts in gearing the city's resources failed due to constant overcrowding and lack of developmental measures including sanitation. The city's main issues, such as poor public health, unemployment, poverty, and maladjustment of unutilized spaces, were evident throughout the twentieth century. This problem still persists today.

Notes

1. John Bellamy Foster, *The Ecological Revolution: Making Peace with the Planet*, New York: Monthly Review Press, 2009, pp. 10–22.
2. Ibid.
3. Narayani Gupta, 'Urban Form and Meaning in South Asia: Perspectives from the Modern Era', *Studies in the History of Art, 1993*, vol. 31, 1993, p. 245.
4. Amiya Kumar Bagchi, *Perilous Passage: Mankind and the Global Ascendency of the Capital*, USA: Rowman and Littlefield, 2005.
5. C.H. Bompas, 'The Work of the Calcutta Improvement Trust', *Journal of the Royal Society of Arts*, vol. 75, no. 3868, 1927, pp. 200–5.

Bibliography

Archival Sources

Annual Report of the Sanitary Commissioner with the Government of India, 1895, Calcutta, 1896.

Annual Report on the Operations of the Calcutta Improvement Trust for the Year 1921–1922, File no. M/3, 1922.

Calcutta High Court, In Re: Manick Chand Mahata vs the Corporation of Calcutta And ... on 16th February, 1921, see url https://indiankanoon.org/doc/1640415, accessed 19 November 2021.

Calcuta Review, vol. XVIII.

Calcutta University Magazine: A Monthly Newspaper and Review, vol. IV, January–December 1897.

Proceedings of the Municipal Department (Sanitation), January, 1911, Proceeding no. 3–4, File no. SE/1, 7th January 1911, Calcutta, 1911.

Proceedings of the Hon'ble the Lieutenant-Government of Bengal, February, 1911 (Municipal Branch), File no. M 1C/2, Proceedings no. B 104–107m, Calcutta, 1911.

Proceedings of the Government of Bengal (Local Self-Government), January 1921, File P.H. 2S-1, Proceedings no. 4–11, Calcutta, 1921,.

Proceedings of the Government of Bengal (Local Self-Government), January, 1921, File no. P.H.Q. -20(1).

The British Medical Journal, vol. 2, no. 1867, October 1896.

The Calcutta Municipal Act 1923, Bengal Act III of 1923, Legislative Department, Government of Bengal, Section 431 and 436.

'The Calcutta University and Science', *Calcutta Review*, 1864.

The Municipal Administrative Reports for the Year 1875–1876 and 1900–1901.

The Calcutta Municipal Act 1923, Section 431 and 436.

The News Page of West Bengal Pollution Control Board, Kolkata.

Published Primary Sources

Bamabodhini Patrika, Ashad 1871 (BS 1278).

Bamabodhini Patrika, Aswin 1893 (BS 1300).

Bamgamahila, Baishakh, vol. I, no. 1, 1875 (BS 1282).

Basu, Parbati, 'Adarsha Grihini', *Bamabodhini Patrika, Falgun*, 1880 (BS 1287).

Bijoli, vol. 16, no. 23, Baishakh/April 1921 (BS 1328).

Chikitsa Sammilani, vol. 8, 1891 (BS 1298).

Chikitshak, vol. 3, no. 4, 1889 (BS 1296).

'Dhatrividya', *Bamabodhini Patrika*, Agrahayan 1867 (BS 1274).

'Garhasthya Shiksha', *Bamabodhini Patrika*, Srabon 1881 (BS 1288).

Ghosh, Ramasundari, 'Samay', *Bamabodhini Patrika*, Kartick 1881 (BS 1288).

'Sharirik Swasthyabidhan', *Bamabodhini Patrika*, Jaisthya 1867 (BS 1274).

'Sishupalan', *Bamabodhini Patrika*, Magh 1869 (BS 1276).

'Sishuder Ahar', *Bamabodhini Patrika*, Baisakh 1866 (BS 1273).

'Sishusantaner prati Matar Kartabya', *Bamabodhini Patrika*, Kartick 1892 (BS 1299).

'Swasthyaraksha', *Bamabodhini Patrika*, Poush 1863 (BS 1270).

'Swasthyaraksha', *Bamabodhini Patrika*, Falgun 1863 (BS 1270).

Swasthya, vol. 3, no. 1, Baishakh/April–May 1899 (BS 1306).

Swasthya Samachar, vol. 1, 1912 (BS 1319).

Swasthya Samachar, vol. 7, Kartick (BS 1319).

Works in Bengali

Bandyopadhyay, Bhabanicharan, *Kalikata Kamalaya*, Calcutta: Ranjana Publishing House, 1951.

Bandyopadhyay, Brajendranath, *Deshiyo Samoyikpatrer Itihas*, vol. I, Kolkata: Ranjan Publishing House and Bangiya Sahitya Parishad, 1935.

———, *Bangla Samoyikpatra*, vol 1, 4th edn., Kolkata: Bangiya Sahitya Parishad, 1972 .

Basu, Swapan and Muntasir Mamun, eds., *Dui Sataker Bangla Sangbad Samoyikpatra*, Kolkata: Pustak Bipani, 2005.

Chattopadhyay, Bankim Chandra, ed., *Bangadarshan*, Bhawanipur: Shri Brajamadhav Basu, 1873.

Chattopadhyay, Debi Prasad, *Lokayata: A Study of Ancient Indian Materialism*, New Delhi: Peoples Publishing House, 2008.

Dutta, Mahendranath, *Kalikatar Puratan Kahini O Protha*, Calcutta: Mahendra Publishing Committee, 1884; repr., 1978.

Ghose, Binay, *Samoyikpatre Banglar Samajchitra*, vol. V, Kolkata: Papyrus, 1983.

Mitra, Peary Chand, *Alaler Gharer Dulal*, 1858; repr., ed. Brajendranath Bandyopadhyay and Sajanikanto Das, Kolkata: Bangiyo Sahitya Parishad, 1993.

Mitra, Radharaman, *Kalikata Darpan*, Parba 1, Calcutta: Subarnalekha, 1952,

Ray, Bharati, *Nari o Paribar: Bamabodhini Patrika*, Kolkata: Pustak Biponi, 1999.

———, *Sekaler Nari Siksha: Bamabodhini Patrika*, Kolkata: Womens Studies Research Centre, Calcutta University, 1994.

Sastri, Sivanath, *Ramtanu Lahiri o Tatkalin Brahmosamaj*, Calcutta: New Age Publishers, 1900.

———, *Grihadharma*, Calcutta: Sadharan Brahmo Samaj, 1889; repr., 1941.

Sengupta, Tanusree, 'Bamabodhini Patrika: Samajbhabna o Sahityaprasanga', unpublished PhD thesis, Santiniketan, Visvabharati, 2012.

Tagore, Rabindranath, *Rachanabali*, 9th khanda, Santiniketan: Visvabharati, BS 1396.

Works in English

Arnold, David, *Colonizing the Body: State Medicine and Epidemic Disease in Nineteenth Century India*, Berkeley: University of California Press, 1993.

———, *Toxic Histories: Poison and Pollution in Modern India*, Cambridge: Cambridge University Press, 2016.

Asdal, Kristin, 'The Problematic Nature of Nature: The Post-Constructivist Challenge to Environmental History', *History and Theory*, vol. 42, no. 4, 2003.

Bagchi, Amiya Kumar, *Perilous Passage: Mankind and the Global Ascendency of the Capital*, UK: Rowman and Littlefield Publishers, 2005.

Bala, Poonam, *Imperialism and Medicine in Bengal: A Socio-Historical Perspective*, New Delhi: Sage Publications, 1991.

Bandyopadhyay, Arun, 'Towards an Understanding of the Environmental History of India', *Calcutta Historical Journal*, vol. XVI, no. 2, July–December 1994.

Banerjee, Sumanta, *Memoirs of Roads: Calcutta from Colonial Urbanization to Global Modernizaton*, New Delhi: Oxford University Press, 2016.

————, *The Wicked City: Crime and Punishment in Colonial Bengal*, New Delhi: Orient Blackswan, 2009.

Basu, Sudipto, 'Spatial Imagination and Development in Colonial Calcutta c. 1850–1900', *History and Sociology of South Asia*, vol. 10, no. 1, 2015, pp. 35–52

Berman, Marshall, *All That is Solid Melts into Air: The Experience of Modernity*, New York: Penguin Books, 1988.

Beverly, H., *Report on the Census of Calcutta*, Calcutta: Bengal Secretariat Press, 1876.

Bhabha, Homi K., *The Location of Culture*, London: Routledge, 1994.

Bhattacharya, Debjani, *Empire and Ecology in Bengal Delta: The Making of Calcutta*, Cambridge: Cambridge University Press, 2018.

Bompas, C.H., 'The Work of the Calcutta Improvement Trust', *Journal of the Royal Society of Arts*, vol. 5, no. 3868, January1927, pp. 200–34.

Borthwick, Meredith, *The Changing Role of Women in Bengal, 1849–1905*, Princeton: Princeton University Press, 1984.

Bose, N.K., *Calcutta: 1964: A Social Survey*, Bombay: Lalvani, 1968.

Bose, Pradip Kumar, ed., *Health and Society in Bengal: A Selection from the late 19th Century Bengali Periodicals*, New Delhi: Thousand Oaks, 2006.

Burton, Antoinette, *Dwelling in the Archive: Women Writing House Home and History in Late Colonial India*, New York: Oxford University Press, 2003.

Busteed, H.E., *Echoes from Old Calcutta*, New Delhi: Asian Educational Services, 1999.

Castells, Manuel, *The City and the Grassroots: A Cross Cultural Theory of Urban Social Movements*, London: Hodder Arnold, 1983.

Chakrabarti, Dipankar 'Calcutta's Environment', in *Calcutta the Living City*, vol II: The Present and Future, ed. Sukanta Chaudhuri, New Delhi: Oxford University Press, 1990, pp. 181–9.

Chakrabarty, Dipesh, 'In Defense of "Provincializing Europe": A Response to Carola Dietze', *History and Theory*, vol. 47, no. 1, February 2008, pp. 85–91.

———, 'Of Garbage, Modernity and the Citizen's Gaze', *Economic and Political Weekly*, March 1992, pp. 541–7.

Chakrabarti, Hiren, ed., *Bengal Past and Present*, Calcutta, Calcutta Historical Society, 1990.

Chakravarti, Pratik, *Bacteriology in British India: Laboratory Medicine and the Tropics*, UK: Boydell and Brewer, 2013.

Chakrabarti, Ranjan, ed., *Critical Themes in Environmental History of India*, New Delhi: Sage, 2020.

Chattopadhyay, Swati, *Representing Calcutta: Modernity, Nationalism and Colonial Uncanny*, UK: Psychology Press, 2005.

Chatterjee, Partha, *The Nation and its Fragments*, New York: Oxford, 1995.

Chatterjee, Monidip, 'Town Planning in Calcutta: Past, Present and Future', in *Calcutta the Living City*, vol II: The Present and Future, ed. Sukanta Chaudhuri, New Delhi: Oxford University Press, 1990, pp. 133–47.

Cotton, H.E.A., *Calcutta Old and New: A Historical and Descriptive Handbook to the City*, Calcutta: W. Newman, 1907.

Das, Apalak, 'Leprosy in Bengal, C. 1873–1956', unpublished PhD dissertation, Kolkata, Jadavpur University, 2021.

Das, Suranjan and Achinyta Kumar Dutta, eds., *Dreadful Diseases in Colonial Bengal: Cholera, Malaria and Smallpox*, Delhi: Primus Books, 2021.

Dasgupta, Subrata, *The Bengal Renaissance: Identity and Creativity from Rammohun Roy to Rabindranath Tagore*, New Delhi: Permanent Black, 2007.

Datta, Partho, *Planning the City: Urbanization and Reform in Calcutta (1800–1940)*, New Delhi: Tulika Books, 2012.

———, 'Calcutta on the Threshold of the 1940s' in *The Stormy Decades: Calcutta*, ed. Tanika Sarkar and Sekhar Bandyopadhyay, New Delhi: Social Science Press, 2015.

Davison, Graeme, 'The City as a Natural System: Theories of Urban Society in Early Nineteenth Century Britain', in *The Pursuit of Urban History*, ed. Detek Fraser and Anthony Sutcliffe, London: E. Arnold, 1983.

Detwyler, Thomas R. and Marvin G. Marcus, eds., *Urbanization and Environment: The Physical Geography of the City*, California: Duxbury Press, 1972.

Dey, Suvankar, 'The Silent Killer: Tuberculosis in Colonial and Post-Colonial Bengal (1911–1962)', unpublished PhD dissertation, Kolkata, Jadavpur University, 2019.

Dhar, Aparajita, 'Women's Writing and Health in Colonial Bengal', in *Murmurs of History: Essays in Honour of Professor Ranjit Sen*, ed. Prasanta K. Mandal and Anjona Chattopadhyay, Kolkata: Progressive Publishers, 2018.

Doughlas, Ian, 'Cities, an Environmental History', in *Environmental History and Global Change*, London: I.B. Tauris, 2013.

Douglas, Mary, *Purity and Danger, An Analysis of Concepts of Pollution and Taboo*, USA: Routledge, 2003.

Dutta, Sweta, *A Social History of the Natural Calamities in Colonial Bengal*, USA: LAP LAMBERT Academic Publishing, 2021.

Foster, John Bellamy, *The Ecological Revolution: Making Peace with the Planet*, New York: Monthly Review Press, 2009.

Furedy, Chris, 'British Tradesmen of Calcutta (1830–1900): A Preliminary Study of their Political and Economic Roles', in *Women Politics and Literature in Bengal*, ed. C.B. Sealy, East Lansing: Asian Studies Center, Michigan State University, 1981, pp. 43–62.

Gadgil, Madhav and Ramachandra Guha, eds., *This Fissured Land: An Ecological History of India*, Berkeley: University of California Press, 1993.

Gandy, Matthew, 'From Urban Ecology to Ecological Urbanism: An Ambiguous Trajectories', *Royal Geographical Society*, vol. 47, no. 2, June 2015, pp. 150–61.

Ghose, Benoy, 'Colonial Beginnings of Calcutta: Urbanisation without Industrialisaton', *The Economic Weekly*, April 1960, pp. 1256–70.

Ghosh, Murari, Alok Dutta, and Biswanath Ray, *Calcutta: A Case Study in Urban-Growth Dynamics*, Calcutta: Firma KLM, 1972.

Ghosh, A.K., *Urban Ecology: A Case Study of Calcutta*, Calcutta: Institute of Local and Urban Studies, Government of West Bengal, 1988.

Ghosh, Anindita, *Claiming the City: Protest, Crime and Scandals in Colonial Calcutta c. 1860–1920*, New Delhi: Oxford University Press, 2016.

Ghosh, Bishwendu, 'From Palki to Automobile: Transport Revolution in Colonial Bengal', unpublished MPhil thesis, Jadavpur University, 2017.

Ghosh, Nabaparna, *A Hygienic City-Nation: Space, Community and Everyday Life in Colonial Calcutta*, Calcutta: Calcutta University Press, 2016.

Goode, S.W., *Municipal Calcutta: Its Institutions in their Growth and Origin*, Edinburgh: The Corporation of Calcutta, T & A Constable, 1916.

Guha, Ramachandra, *The Unquiet Woods: Ecological Change and Peasant Resistance in the Himalaya*, Berkley: University of California Press, 2000.

Guha, Sumit, *Health and Population in South Asia From Earliest Times to the Present*, Ranikhet: Permanent Black, 2010.

Guha, Supriya, 'The Nature of Women: Medical Ideas in Colonial Bengal', *Indian Journal of Gender Studies*, vol. 3, no. 1, 1996, pp. 23–38.

Gupta, Narayani 'Urban Form and Meaning in South Asia: Perspectives from the Modern Era', *Studies in the History of Art, 1993*, vol. 31, 1993, pp. 243–52.

Harrison, Mark, *Climate and Constitutions: Health, Race, Environment and British Imperialism in India, 1600–1850*, New Delhi: Oxford University Press, 1999.

———, *Public Health in British India: Anglo-Indian Preventive Medicine, 1859–1914*, Cambridge: Cambridge University Press, 1994.

Harvey, David, *Social Justice and the City*, USA: Georgia University Press: 1973.

Havlick, Spenser W., *The Urban Organism: The City's Natural Resources from an Environmental Perspective*, New York: Macmillan, 1974.

Hays, Samuel P., *Conservation and the Gospel of Efficiency: The Progressive Conservation Movement, 1890–1920*, USA: University of Pittsburgh Press, 1959; repr., 1999.

———, 'Hundred Years of the University of Calcutta', Calcutta: University of Calcutta Press, 1957.

Jana, Nandini, 'Towards Writing a History of Women in the Brahmo Samaj, 1872–1921', unpublished PhD dissertation, Kolkata, Jadavpur University, 2018.

Jeffery, Roger, *The Politics of Health in India*, Berkeley: University of California Press, 1988.

King, Anthony D., *Colonial Urban Development: Culture, Social Power and Environment*, London: Routledge, 1976.

Kumar, Deepak, *Science and the Raj: A Study of the British India*, New Delhi: Oxford University Press, 2006.

———— and Raj Sekhar Basu, eds., *Medical Encounters in British India*, New Delhi: Oxford University Press, 2013.

Lanchester, H.V., 'Calcutta Improvement Trust: Precis of Mr. E.P. Richards' Report on the City of Calcutta', *The Town Planning Review*, vol. 5, no. 3, October 1914.

Lefebvre, Henri, *The Production of Space*, Oxford: Blackwell, 1991.

Majumdar, Aishwaryarupa, 'Medical Education on the Colonial Periphery: A Study of the Medical Institutions in Patna and Dacca', *Indian Journal of History of Science*, vol. 53, no. 1, 2018, pp. 33– 47.

Melosi, Martin V., 'The Place of the City in Environmental History', *Environmental Review,* vol. 111, 1979, pp. 37–45.

Mitra, Asok, *Calcutta Diary*, Great Britain: Frank Cass and Co. Ltd., 1977.

Mitra, Manimanjari, *Calcutta in the 20th Century: An Urban Disaster*, Calcutta: Asiatic Book Agency, 1990.

Mukharji, Prajit Bihari, *Nationalizing the Body: The Medical Market and Daktari Medicine*, Kolkata: Anthem Press, 2009.

Mukherjee, Rila, 'The Making of Maritime Economy: Bengal, 1600–1800', in *A Comprehensive History of Modern Bengal, 1700–1950*, vol. I, ed. Sabyasachi Bhattacharya, Delhi: Primus Books, 2020, pp. 164–211.

Mukherjee, S.N., *Calcutta: Myths and Histories*, Calcutta: Subarnarekha, 1977.

Mukherjee, Sujata, *Gender, Medicine and Society in Colonial India*, New Delhi: Oxford University Press, 2017.

Mukherji, Trailakya Nath, and Amrita Lal Sircar, eds., *Indian Association for the Cultivation of Science: Its Short Histories and Urgent Needs*, Calcutta: Anglo-Sanskrit Press, 1903.

Mumford, Lewis, *The City in History: Its Origins, Its Transformations and Its Prospects*, New York: MJF Books, 1961.

Nash, Roderick, *Wilderness and the American Mind*, New Haven: Yale University Press, 1973.

Nair, P.T., ed., *Job Charnock: The Founder of Calcutta: In Facts and Fiction: An Anthology*, Calcutta: Calcutta Old Book Stall, 1977.

———, *Calcutta in the 17th Century*, Kolkata: Firma KLM, 1986.

———, *Calcutta in the 18th century*, Kolkata: Firma KLM, 1984.

———, *Calcutta in the 19th Century: Company's Days*, Kolkata: Firma KLM, 1989.

———, *Calcutta: Origin of the Name*, Calcutta: Subarnarekha, 1985.

———, 'Civic and Public Services in Old Calcutta', in *Calcutta: The Living City*, vol I: The Past, ed. Sukanta Chaudhuri, New Delhi: Oxford University Press, 1990, pp. 224–37.

Pati, Biswamoy and Mark Harrison, eds., *The Social History of Health and Medicine in Colonial India*, New York: Routledge, 2009.

Palit, Chittabrata and Achintya Dutta, eds., *The History of Medicine in India: The Medical Encounter*, New Delhi: Kalpaz, 2005.

Palit, Chittabrata and Mahua Sarkar, eds., *Indian Vistas of Environment*, New Delhi: Kalpaz, 2007.

Porter, Roy, *Disease, Medicine and Society in England, 1550–1860*, London: Macmillan, 2009.

Prasad, Srirupa, *Cultural Politics of Hygiene in India (1890–1940)*, UK: Palgrave Macmillan, 2015.

Pratt, Mary Louis, *Imperial Eyes: Travel Writing and the Transculturation*, London, Routledge: 1992.

Raina, Dhruv and S. Irfan Habib, eds., *Domesticating Modern Science: A Social History of Science and*

Culture in Modern India, New Delhi: Tulika Books, 2004.

Rainbow, P., ed., *The Foucault Reader*, New York: Pantheon Books, 1984.

Rainey, H. James, *Historical and Topographical Sketch of Calcutta*, Calcutta: Englishman Press, 1876.

Ramasubban, Radhika, *Public Health and Medical Research in India: Their Origins and Development under the Impact of British Colonial Policy*, Stockholm: SAREC, 1982.

Ray, Kabita, *History of Public Health: Colonial Bengal (1921–1947)*, Kolkata: K.P. Bagchi and Co., 1998.

Ray, Rajat Kanta, 'Civil Society and Politics: Bengal (1905–1927)', in *A Comprehensive History of Modern Bengal, 1700–1950*, vol. III, ed. Sabyasachi Bhattacharya, New Delhi: Primus Books, 2020, pp. 231–312.

Roy, Biren, *Marshes to Metropolis: Calcutta, 1481–1981*, Calcutta: National Council of Education, 1982.

Roy, Tirthankar, *India in the World Economy from Antiquity to the Present*, UK: Cambridge University Press, 2012.

Samanta, Arabinda, *Living with Epidemics in Colonial Bengal*, New Delhi: Manohar, 2017.

Sarkar, Mahua, ed., *Environment and History: Recent Dialogues*, New Delhi: Kalpaz, 2007.

———, *A Collage of Environmental History*, Kolkata and New Delhi: Alphabet Books and Manohar, 2017.

———, *Environment and the Adivasi World*, Kolkata and New Delhi: Alphabet Books and Manohar, 2017.

———, *Historical Essays in Memory of Professor Subhasis Biswas: Themes in Science, Technology, Environment and Medicine*, Kolkata and New Delhi: Alphabet Books and Manohar, 2021.

———, 'Pollution, Public Health and the People of Calcutta: The Nineteenth Century', *Journal of the Asiatic Society*, vol. LXII, no. 4, 2020, pp. 85–107.

————— and Subhasis Biswas, eds., *Glimpses of Environmental History*, Kolkata: Alphabet Books, 2018.

Sarkar, Sumit, *Modern Times (India, 1880s–1950s): Environment, Economy, Culture*, New Delhi: Permanent Black, 2014.

Sarkar, Suvobrata, 'The Electrification of Colonial Calcutta: Role of the Innovators, Bureaucrats and Foreign Business Organizations, 1880–1940', *Studies in History*, vol. 34, no. 1, 2017, pp. 48–76.

—————, *Let there be Light: Engineering, Entrepreneurship and Electricity in Colonial Bengal, (1880–1945)*, London: Cambridge University Press, 2020.

Sen, S.N, 'The Pioneering Role of Calcutta in Scientific and Technical Education in India', *Indian Journal of History of Science*, vol. 29, no. 1, 1994, pp. 41–7.

Sheard, Sally and Hellen Power, *Body and City: Histories of Urban Public Health*, United Kingdom: Ashgate, 2000.

Sinha, Pradip, *Calcutta in Urban History*, Calcutta: Firma KLM, 1978.

Index

9 789356 870710